All About the Sea

allabout
books

By Ferdinand C. Lane

Author of The Mysterious Sea

Illustrated by Fritz Kredel

This special edition is printed and distributed by
arrangement with the originators and publishers of
Allabout Books, RANDOM HOUSE, Inc., New York, by

E. M. HALE AND COMPANY
EAU CLAIRE, WISCONSIN

Contents

That Wonderland— The Sea

How the Sea Began

Long ago when our world was young, there was no
sea. There was neither land nor water as we know them
now, for the earth was slowly taking shape out of such
stuff as the stars are made of. This stuff is made up of
many things called elements. There are nearly a hundred
of them. The lighter ones are called gases. Some of these
form the air we breathe.

The heavier ones have sunk into the earth. The center

of the earth is a great core of iron. Around this core, like the layers on an onion, lighter substances have collected. That is why metals like lead and gold are so scarce upon the surface. That is why light metals like aluminum or the silicon which forms our windowpanes are so common.

Some scientists believe that our world grew slowly, bit by bit, out of matter that floats in space like dust specks in a sunbeam. There are such bits of matter. We call them shooting stars, and sometimes we see them at night blazing in the upper air. A few, large enough to reach the earth, are called meteors. They are formed of metals, mainly iron or rock much like those on the earth.

Most scientists have thought that our world was formed in a different way. They think it was torn away from the great central mass that was to be the sun. It went whirling off into the sky. And as it whirled, it slowly became more round and solid. It was so hot that it glowed like a burning coal. As it cooled, it began to shrink just as a baked apple cools and shrinks until its smooth skin wrinkles into folds and hollows. In the same way the earth's skin, that we call the crust, formed folds and hollows. The larger folds became the continents. The hollows became the beds of seas.

There was another reason for these folds and hollows.

Heavier rocks sank deeper into the soft earth's crust. Lighter rocks rose to the surface. And so the continents are mainly granite, a lighter rock than the heavier basalt that forms so much of the ocean floor.

In this way the beds were hollowed out for the seas although there were no seas then. The earth was much too hot. If we spill water on a hot stove, the drops only dash about, then rise in steam. So it was with the heated earth.

Where did all the water come from that now fills the seas? Some scientists believe that it formed deep in the cooling earth and has been forming there ever since.

Water is made up of two gases, the oxygen that we take in with every breath, and hydrogen, the lightest of all known elements. We cannot see hydrogen, but we can watch it burning with a blue flame on a coal or oil stove. Far down among the rocks these two gases unite to form water. It rises in hot springs and from those "fire mountains" that we call volcanoes. So we are told that just such water slowly filled the deeper hollows in the earth's crust where we now have seas.

Other scientists believe that the seas once floated in dense clouds that filled the sky. As these cooled, they poured forth rain. It must have rained not for days or

It must have rained for thousands of years,

weeks but for thousands of years. The mind cannot grasp such storms as roared about the infant world. Even when the seas were filled, they must have raged and foamed for a long time. Their waves gnawed at the shores of the continents that were rising as the earth's crust wrinkled more and more. Many long ages must have passed before either sea or land became fixed in anything like their present form.

We cannot be too sure just when the seas were born. For even the wisest men do not always agree on what happened so long ago.

How long, you ask? Those who know best tell us that this world of ours is more than two billion years old. That is a number that takes our breath away. What is a billion? No one knows. It is so big that our minds cannot grasp it. To be sure, we know that our government spends billions of dollars every year. We are also told that more than two billion people now live upon this earth. We talk in billions, but we could not count one if we spent our whole lifetime in doing it.

Men who are trained for such work study the rocks which have been laid down in great sheets over much of the dry land. Some of these sheets are sandstone. This is made up of older rocks ground down by the seas or the winds and then turned into rock again. Some of them are shale or slate. This is fine clay that formed in the bottom of lakes or in inlets from the sea and was pressed into stone. Some are limestone made up of the shells of tiny creatures that once lived in the sea. Some of them even show the print of leaves that grew on trees millions of years ago, or the bones of creatures that lived and died and have disappeared forever.

Scientists read these sheets of rock one by one as you read the pages of a printed book. They notice how fast the mountains are worn away by frost and wind and rain. They see how slowly valleys and other low places fill up. They even try to find out how long it must have taken the sea to become as salty as it is today. These and other things they add together line by line. And the picture they trace, though dim, grows ever clearer. It is the picture of a world that began more than two billion years ago.

Long ages after the earth had wrinkled into folds and hollows and had cooled enough, water flowed into those hollows. The sea is younger than the earth. But it is very old. It is older than the mountains and the continents we know today. Some of them may be formed upon the first great folds of the earth's crust. But if so, they have changed so much through the ages that they seem very different now. Their rocks have crumbled into sand or dust to be pressed into different kinds of rock again and again. Or melted rock, called lava, has bubbled up from deep down in the earth to become solid rock once more.

But water is always water. It rises from the sea in clouds only to return to the sea in rain drops or in rivers. And so, while islands rise and fall, and the outlines of the continents swell or shrink from age to age, the sea remains the sea. It is the one surface of the ancient world which has changed the least.

How the Sea Is Divided

Today most of our earth is hidden by the sea. All the continents and islands form less than a third of its surface. Strange to say, we can see the face of the full moon more clearly than that of the world on which we live. Bright spots and dark shadows show her mountains and her valleys. But no one has ever seen the mountains and the valleys that lie buried under the sea. Ours is a world of water far more than a world of land.

There is much water in our lakes and rivers. It is in the clouds above us, in the air we breathe, and in the

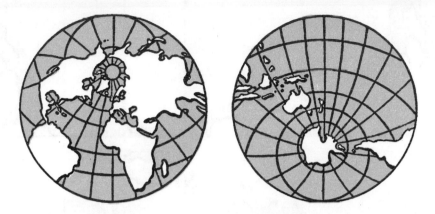

Ours is a world of water far more than a world of land.

ground beneath our feet. But almost all the water in the world, or ninety-five per cent, is in the sea.

It is easy to divide the land into farms or city lots. It is not so easy to divide the sea. But to help us in finding places on the map, the sea has been marked off into three main parts called oceans.

Best known of these is the Atlantic. The old Greeks called it that in honor of the Giant Atlas. They thought he stood upon the shore of Africa where snow-capped peaks now rise. He was so tall and strong that he carried the sky upon his shoulders as he looked out into the sea which lay before him. Our geography book or atlas, as it is sometimes called, was also named for this giant.

The Indian Ocean seems to have gained its name in

GREENLAND

SPITZBERGEN

White
Sea

ICELAND

Baltic Sea

E U R O P E

Black Sea

Atlantic

Mediterranean Sea

Persian Gulf

Indus

WEST
INDIES

Red Sea

INDIA

Caribbean Sea

Ocean

A F R I C A

Bay
of
Bengal

SOUTH
AMERICA

Indian
Ocean

a strange way, from the Indus River and the Land of India through which it flows.

The Pacific Ocean was first called so by Magellan, who led the first expedition that ever sailed around the world. It seemed so smooth compared with the rough Atlantic, which he had just crossed, that he named it the Pacific, meaning peaceful.

Sometimes two other oceans are also listed, the Arctic and Antarctic. But the Arctic is really a part of the Atlantic. The Antarctic, which lies on the other side of the globe, has no true bounds and is better divided among the three great oceans.

Of these the Pacific is much the largest. It is nearly as large as the Atlantic and Indian Oceans together. It stretches for 10,000 miles, or nearly halfway around the world. It could cover all the continents and islands with millions of square miles to spare.

Next in size is the Atlantic. Though much narrower than the Pacific, it is longer from north to south. This is because it includes the North Pole at one end of the earth and stretches all the way to the Antarctic continent where we find the South Pole.

Smallest of the three is the Indian Ocean. Though very wide, it is not so long as the others, for it is enclosed by the three continents—Africa, Asia and Australia.

These oceans all measure many millions of square miles. But if we give to each a smaller number, the Pacific 12, the Atlantic 7, and the Indian Ocean 5, we shall know as much as we need to know of how they compare in size.

Some parts of these oceans, which are cut off by points of land or by islands, are called seas. Best known is the Mediterranean Sea which separates Europe, Asia and Africa. Many nations grew up along its shores such as Egypt, Judea, Greece and Rome. In this country we often think of the Caribbean Sea, which holds the West Indies, and the Bering Sea, which divides our own Alaska from Russian territory.

The oceans are mainly blue. Sometimes they may look gray under cloudy skies or seem green in shallows where the sandy bottom shows through.

But some seas have been named because they were partly colored by the rivers which flow into them, or by ice, or by tiny plants and animals which live in their waters. So we have the Yellow Sea in China, the White Sea in northern Russia, the Black Sea and the Red Sea.

Some arms of the oceans are also called gulfs like the Gulf of Mexico and the Gulf of California or the Persian

Gulf. There are bays like Hudson Bay and the Bay of Bengal off India and many smaller straits and inlets. They are somewhat like our towns and counties and states which are really parts of one great country. For all such waters, as well as the three big oceans, are only parts of one great sea.

The Rise and Fall of Continents

When we visit the seashore, we stand where land and ocean meet. But this has not always been so. For the line that divides them is always changing. It is a battle line, for the waves and the rocks are at war. Along the eastern coasts of England whole villages have fallen into the sea. In Holland, dikes are built to keep back the sea, and windmills pump out the water. But several hundred years ago the ocean broke through and drowned dozens of Dutch villages. Holland is a low-lying country of sand

In Holland much of the land is below sea level.

and swamp where the pounding sea has the advantage.

But even the strongest cliffs of stone crumble before the waves driven on by winter gales. In Denmark you may even visit a church with one end hanging over the edge of a steep cliff where the sea has eaten into the land.

In many parts of the world, islands have been swallowed up and others have risen in that war of wind and waves which is always going on. And the very continents have changed their size and outlines.

Sometimes these continents, rising as the earth's crust wrinkled more and more, have beaten back the sea. Sometimes the seas have won and flooded great areas of the land. Maps have been made which try to show us what our world looked like 100 million years ago or 500 million. Most of North America once lay beneath the sea. Only eastern Canada, with some of the frozen islands of the Arctic and parts of our own states of New York, Michigan, Wisconsin and Minnesota were then dry land.

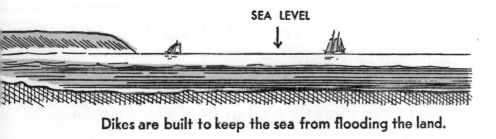

SEA LEVEL

Dikes are built to keep the sea from flooding the land.

All About the Sea

About that time, or perhaps a little later, some parts of South America, Asia and Australia also appeared above the waves. Gradually they took on something like their present shape.

There were many later changes. Not long ago, as scientists reckon time, North America was joined with Asia. Then the Indians, who were our first settlers, could cross Bering Strait on dry land. About the same time the British Isles were a part of Europe. That great desert of Africa that we call the Sahara once formed the bed of a shallow sea. Other seas stretched far across Asia. The valley of the Mississippi has been buried several times by the sea, and a deep gulf once marked the place where the Rocky Mountains now rise.

North of the equator, which divides our earth into two equal parts, the land was more successful in its battle with the sea. North America, Asia, Europe and much of Africa and South America lie north of that line. But even there the sea covers the greater part of the earth's surface.

Only a third of all the dry land lies below the equator. There the world is mostly sea.

Highest of the continents is Antarctica which rises more than a mile above the sea. Lowest of all is Australia.

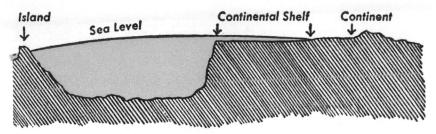

The continental shelves slope gently from the shoreline.

The average height of all the islands and the continents is about half a mile. But there are great areas which are not much above sea level and some that lie below.

Every continent is surrounded by bands of shallow water. These are called the continental shelves. They are the foundations upon which the continents rest. The houses we live in are built upon foundations buried in the ground. The continents are built upon foundations buried in the sea.

The continental shelves are often nearly level, but they mark a gentle slope from the shoreline out to the edge. Once there they dip sharply two miles or more down to the ocean floor. This slope may be steeper than the sides of a mountain or the roof of a house. The average depth of water on the continental shelves is something over 400 feet. Yet around Antarctica it may be 2,000 feet and still remain a true shelf compared with the deep sea beyond.

They may include whole seas like the Baltic Sea or the Persian Gulf. They may unite island groups with a nearby continent, like Great Britain and Europe.

A few coasts have no such shelves. Instead cliffs rise sharply from the deep sea. In others the shelves may be hundreds of miles wide. Their average width is about thirty miles. In many ways they are the most important part of the sea as we shall find in our study of ocean life.

Mountains Under the Sea

We think of mountains rising high above the earth. Some of them are so lofty that even in summer their peaks are covered with snow. A mountain standing all alone above fairly level ground is a grand sight. The Japanese are proud of such a mountain which they call Fujiyama. There are many exquisitely beautiful mountains in the world.

More often mountains are found in groups like the Adirondacks or the Catskills of New York or in long ridges like the Great Smokies of North Carolina or the Sierras of California. The Andes are the longest range of mountains on any continent. They stretch all the way

Mount Fujiyama can be seen for a hundred miles at sea.

from the shores of the Caribbean Sea to bleak Cape Horn at the very southern tip of South America.

But they are not the longest mountain range in the world. That range lies mostly buried beneath the sea. It is called the Mid-Atlantic Ridge. From a point about as far north as Iceland it extends far to the south toward Antarctica. It lies about halfway between Europe and Africa on the one hand and North and South America on the other. It is shaped something like the letter S, and it is more than 10,000 miles long.

Although this great mountain range rises from one to two miles above the ocean floor, most of its peaks are buried beneath water from half a mile to a mile deep. Yet they are true mountains. Many of them are as steep

Island peaks were seen by sailors searching for whales.

and lofty as those much better known upon the land.

In a few places this great range appears above the waves. Its highest point is the island of Pico in the Azores which belong to Portugal. This peak rises more than 7,000 feet above the sea, but from the ocean floor it rears upward more than five miles. Only a few mountains in Asia are higher than this lonely summit away out there in the Atlantic.

Still stranger are St. Paul's Rocks which are about half-way between Brazil and Africa. During some great up-heaval in the earth's crust they came up sheer and steep from the ocean floor. No one knows how or when. Far to the south are other island peaks of the Mid-Atlantic Ridge. As these are washed by the icy waters of the Polar

Sea few people visit them except seamen searching for whales. Their only inhabitants are seals and sea birds.

This great ridge was discovered more than a hundred years ago by scientists who were sounding the depth of the sea. In recent years ships from several countries have explored the range and learned more about it. They have measured the slope of some of its mountains and have brought up sand and pieces of rock. But we still know very little of this longest of all mountain ranges.

The other oceans have nothing quite so impressive, but they do have higher peaks. The big volcano Mauna Kea on the island of Hawaii rises almost 14,000 feet above the sea. But it also thrusts upward from the floor of the Pacific through 16,000 feet of water. So its real height is nearly 30,000 feet or higher than Mount Everest.

Even more interesting are other volcanoes that have never reached the surface. There is such a volcano off the coast of California. Its height has been measured and the depth of its crater, but no one has ever seen it. For its peak lies buried a half-mile or more below the waves. When that volcano erupted and the ash and melted lava poured out, the seas above it must have boiled and great clouds of steam risen high above the waves.

There are other mountains below the sea that are very different. They are flat-topped like the mesas of New Mexico or Table Mountain in South Africa. But their sides are often steep. They are thought to be very old, far older than any mountain now on dry land.

The storms of tens of millions of years have worn down the peaks of the Green Mountains of Vermont and the Blue Ridge. Even the Alps of Switzerland are only the roots of older mountains. Beneath the sea no frosts or driving rains wear the rocks away or fill the valleys. So it is thought that the oldest mountains in the world are these strange flat-topped peaks that no one has ever climbed or even seen.

Exploring the Ocean Floor

There are other things about the ocean floor that we should know, for nearly three-quarters of the face of the earth is ocean floor.

How would you like to take a stroll along the bottom of the sea? No one has ever done this, and it seems hardly likely that anyone ever will. But we may do so in fancy just as we might roam among the mountains of the moon or take a rocket ship to the planet Mars.

Divers may go down hundreds of feet to examine sunken ships.

To be sure, we may all walk a little way across the ocean floor when we follow the ebbing tide across wet rocks and sands. Divers have gone down for many feet after pearls or sponges or searching for wrecks or buried treasure. But these are shallow waters along the continental shelves or near islands. Beyond lies the deep sea. Three-quarters of that sea is at least two miles deep. Half of it is three miles deep or more.

Once we thought that the floor of the deep sea was mostly level, broken only by gentle slopes. Now we know better. Besides the mountain ranges and lonely peaks which are so interesting, the ocean floor rises in great plateaus and sinks into deep valleys.

Many people have thought that the largest of these underwater plateaus mark the places where continents have sunk beneath the waves. The Greeks told such stories of the lost Atlantis which stretched far out into the Atlantic. They thought that island groups off the coast of Africa were all that was left of this drowned continent.

One great plateau beneath the sea reaches across the Indian Ocean from India to lonely Antarctica. Some scientists have said that this plateau is the bed of another lost continent. They have even claimed that southern India and the big island of Madagascar off the coast of Africa were parts of this lost continent.

Still another vast plateau stretches beneath the Pacific from Antarctica to Central America. There are many islands scattered over this part of the ocean. They have been pictured as mountain peaks rising above a lost continent called Mu.

Many scientists believe that the moon was once a part of the earth. Some have thought that the bed of the Pacific was a vast scar upon the face of the earth left when the moon tore loose and went whirling off into the sky.

The Pacific is not only the largest of the oceans, but it is the deepest. The Atlantic is the shallowest, but this is because it includes so great an area of continental shelves.

In addition to the main plateaus under the sea there are many smaller ones. Some of these are called *banks*. The Grand Banks off the coast of Newfoundland are well known. These are larger than Newfoundland itself. Fishermen come all the way from Europe for the cod

Mountain peaks and plateaus lie under the sea.

which are so plentiful in the waters of the Grand Banks.

Another such spot is the Dogger Bank in the North Sea, also famous for its fish. Stone tools and weapons are sometimes dredged up from the Dogger Bank showing that men once lived there when it was dry land, long before written history began.

Quite as interesting as the plateaus and shallows are the deep valleys under the sea. There are gorges, too. One of these has just been traced for more than 800 miles along the floor of the Atlantic. Its steep walls are several hundred feet high.

But there are much deeper valleys that are called *troughs* or *trenches* or *deeps*. We might expect to find them far out in the ocean, but they are usually quite near the land. The deepest part of the Atlantic lies not far off

From woodcut by Hokusai

Puerto Rico. The deepest spot in the Indian Ocean is near the island of Java.

The Pacific has deeper troughs and trenches. One of these lies off the coast of Japan. But the German cruiser *Emden* found a deeper spot about forty miles from the shore of Mindanao in the Philippines. Here the sounding line ran out 35,400 feet, or more than six miles and a half. These figures have since been reduced a bit and a still deeper spot reported near the island of Guam. But the Pacific is so big that even greater depths may yet be found.

Even the shallows along the coastline have their deep places. These are canyons which stretch from near the shore out to the edge of the continental shelf where it plunges to the ocean floor. There is such a canyon off Monterey in California. Its walls are steeper and rise higher than the walls of the Grand Canyon of the Colorado. Similar gorges have been found off the mouth of the Hudson River, off the Congo in Africa, and in other places. And so if we go sailing in a boat along the shore, we may be passing over some steep valley that would attract people from all over the world if it could be seen.

Just what carved these buried canyons we do not know. Some scientists think they were dredged by rivers when the continents rose higher than they do today. Others think they were gouged out by the ice in what we shall learn was once the Ice Age. Still others believe they are only cracks in the earth's crust. Whatever caused them, they are the strangest of all the strange landscapes that lie hidden beneath the sea.

Those Children of the Winds — the Waves

The surface of a pond is often still. It reflects trees and houses like a mirror. But the sea is never still. Its waters are always in motion. And among those motions the simplest and the easiest to understand are the waves.

When you blow upon a plate of soup to cool it, you make tiny waves. That is what happens when storm winds blow upon the sea. Few sights are grander than a rocky shore where the great waves come rolling in. How they foam and splash! How they roar until the very windows rattle!

But if you saw something floating out there and waited for it to come within reach, you might be disappointed. For it would only bob up and down without getting much closer. That is just what every drop of water in

Arctic tern   Dovekies   Puffin

the wave would be doing. Up and down and around it would go as though dancing gaily with the winds.

Tie one end of a rope to a tree. You can send wave after wave along the rope, but the rope itself will stay where you hold it. So it is with the sea. Wave motions pass through the water tossing it up and down, but there is little or no forward movement. Only when the wave nears the land, it trips and pitches forward just as you might do if you caught your toe on the edge of a rug. Then it curls over and sprawls ahead in a rush of foam.

The top of the wave is called its *crest*. The hollow between two waves is called the *trough*. And the distance from trough to crest is the height of the wave.

To the person on the shore that is the only thing that matters. But far out at sea waves are also measured in other ways. There is the *speed* of the wave motion through the water. A common speed is fifteen miles an hour. But wave motions caused by earthquakes have traveled through the sea faster than a jet plane can go.

Another measurement is the distance between waves. This is called the *interval*. As waves approach the land, they crowd together and almost tumble over one another. They are like people hurrying out of a movie theater. But away off at sea, where there is plenty of room, waves may be hundreds of feet apart.

Sailors also speak of the *fetch* of a wave. By that they mean the distance that the wave motion has traveled through the water. It may have come from somewhere hundreds or even thousands of miles away.

Really big waves need elbowroom. One that is 5 feet high near shore might be 15 feet high 100 miles at sea. Out in mid-ocean we may look for those moving hills of water that make such a ship as the *Queen Elizabeth* toss about like a chip in a rapid brook.

A sudden squall may "kick up" what sailors call a "choppy sea." But only gales that blow for days stir up such foaming hills of water. They are the "gray beards" off Cape Horn that sailors used to dread.

There are other regions where waves are high. Such is the North Atlantic in winter and the seas around Antarctica. Another is the Cape of Good Hope near the southern tip of Africa. It was first named the Cape of Storms.

Waves breaking on the shore have enormous power. One twelve feet high may strike with a force of more than a hundred tons for every foot of its length. In the English town of Wick a great block of cement weighing 2,600 tons was clamped to solid rock by iron rods three inches thick to form a breakwater. But it was torn loose by the waves in a storm in 1877.

This prehistoric fish was 20 feet long and a great fighter.

All About the Sea

Waves are also great climbers. They race up a sloping shore driven by the force of the sea behind them until they may mount 300 feet or more.

In the Faroe Islands north of Scotland, waves have lifted a rock weighing 40 tons 160 feet above the sea.

Greatest of all waves are those caused by volcanoes or by earthquakes. In 1883 Krakatoa erupted off the shores of Java, halfway around the world. Waves rose 100 feet or more and drowned 20,000 people on nearby coasts. These waves crossed the Pacific at a speed of 700 miles an hour and broke in tiny wavelets in San Francisco Bay. In 1946 a part of the ocean floor gave way off the coast of the Aleutian Islands in Alaska. This made great waves that were thought to be ninety miles apart! In five hours they reached Hawaii where they did much damage.

Yet, destructive as they are, the waves have carved our seacoasts into lovely rock spires and caves and beaches.

Along many shores, even in calm weather, great waves may roll in from the sea for days at a time. They are called ocean *swells*. They have been caused by winds hundreds of miles away. Stations have been built on some coasts to study them, for they often foretell coming storms.

Most waves do not reach very far below the surface.

But deep down are other even larger waves. They are found in places where ocean currents clash or where saltier meets fresher sea water. We know little about them except their action upon submarines. They are one of the many mysterious things that the sea hides from our view.

The Unseen Pull of Sun and Moon

On our first visit to the seashore we might wonder most of all at other strange movements in the sea. These are called the tides. For some hours the water goes away leaving rocks or sand bars bare. Then it comes slowly back to bury them again. The outgoing water is called the *ebb*, the incoming water the *flow*. And along most coasts the sea ebbs and flows twice in a little more than twenty-four hours.

The tides are really enormous waves. Most waves along the shore rise and fall every few moments and only ruffle the surface. But the tides rise and fall for hours and reach clear down to the bottom of the sea.

People have always been puzzled by the tides. Once they feared the earth itself was breathing like some great monster. Julius Caesar thought the moon had something

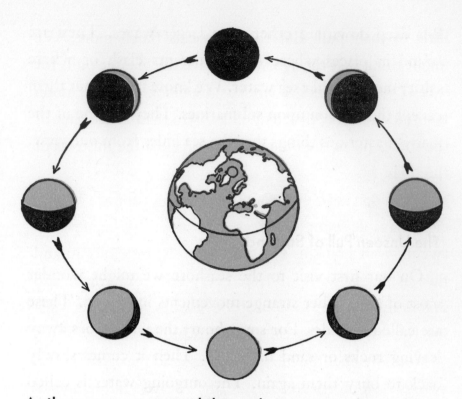

As the moon moves around the earth, it seems to change shape.

to do with the tides. And he was right, though he did not know just why.

Hold up a stone, then let go and it will fall to the ground. That is because the earth attracts it just as you may have seen a magnet draw bits of iron to itself. All matter obeys this law which is called gravity.

The sun and moon far off in space are always pulling at the earth like great magnets. Even the rocks yield a little to their pull. But the sea yields much more. We might think that the sun would have the greater pull, for it is 27 million times as large as the moon. But the moon is so much nearer that its pull is more than twice that of the sun. And so the moon has been called the mistress of the tides.

The moon revolves around the earth in about twenty-eight days dragging the tides after it. But there are only twenty-four hours in a day. And so the time of ebb and flow is nearly an hour later every day. Fishermen and sailors and summer visitors at the beaches are always waiting for this changing time in the tides.

Not only does the moon travel around the earth. It also swings from north to south of the equator. Sometimes it is nearer and sometimes farther away. So its pull upon the sea always changes. Besides, the sun is also pulling. When moon and sun are right in line, their pull is greater. Often they are pulling in different directions. And so the tides are sometimes very high and at other times much lower.

The motion of the tides also depends upon the outline of the land. In mid-ocean they may rise and fall only a foot or two. In many bays and inlets the difference may be many feet.

When the tide comes in, water rises in the bay.

The highest tides in the world sweep into the Bay of Fundy in Nova Scotia. There they rise more than fifty feet. A tall ship at anchor is left high and dry on the beach to float once more when the tide comes in. The Bay of Fundy is shaped like a funnel. The water pouring into this funnel is driven into a narrow space so that it rises higher and higher.

Some other places in the world have tides of more than thirty feet. A few rivers like the Amazon push back the sea a little. But when the tide turns, it rushes upstream in a great wave that may be ten feet high or more. For the sea is much stronger than any river.

At ebb tide, the water level falls, leaving a sandy beach.

There are a few places where the sun rather than the moon seems to control the tides. This is true in the beautiful island of Tahiti in the Pacific. Manila is one place which has only one tide a day instead of two. And there are places which have scarcely any tide at all.

For other forces besides the pull of sun and moon affect the tides. Strangest of these are the *seiches*. If you carry a pan full of water, it will spill very easily. The water swings first to one side then the other. And we find just such movements in partly enclosed seas. We call these movements *seiches*.

Philippine natives speak of the Crazy Tides of Palawan

which may rise four feet or more. Every fifty minutes or so the waters of the Sulu Sea slop from side to side like a great pan of water. There are seiches in Long Island Sound and many other places.

It is thought that much larger areas of the oceans act in the same way. We find little tide motion at their centers, a greater rise and fall at their edges.

Just what causes seiches is still in doubt. It is thought that they are due to changes in air pressure. For they are also found in many lakes as well as in the sea.

We do know that air pressure has some influence upon the tides. Let the barometer fall an inch, and the tide may rise a foot. There is less weight of air upon it to hold it down. Strong winds may do much more. The hurricane of 1938 drove the waters of Narragansett Bay ten feet above high water mark to flood part of the city of Providence.

The problem of the tides is never quite the same at any two places. And it changes with every passing hour. Yet machines have been invented that can tell you just what the pull of sun and moon will be anywhere in the world a year in advance. It takes the machine about seven hours to answer such a question. Even then it cannot tell you how the winds or the barometer will act on that day.

Tides are important in every seaport. In many of them the biggest ships must wait for high tide to enter or leave the harbor. Among islands on rocky coasts tides often cause swift currents that can be dangerous. They may even form great whirlpools. The most famous whirlpool in the world is off the coast of Norway. It is called the Maelstrom. Sailors once thought that it would swallow big ships. Thrilling stories have been written about this whirlpool.

Tides pouring in and out of enclosed bays once turned mill wheels to grind grain and cut timber in New England. Even the Government has tried to harness the tide in Passamaquoddy Bay in Maine. There two billion tons of water rush in and out with every tide.

Long ago, when the world was young, the tides were much higher than they are now. The earth then turned upon its axis once in four hours instead of twenty-four as it does now. The moon was also much nearer. And so tides hundreds of feet high raced around the world foaming over the continents that were just appearing above the sea.

That is a long look into the past. But a look into the future is quite as strange. For the tides act like a brake upon the spinning earth. The power that controls them comes from the far-off sun and moon. Their steady pull is slowing up the spin of the earth just as a magnet will slow a spinning wheel. This will go on until the day once four hours long will lengthen to about twenty-eight days.

And what a difference that will make in our climate! For the sun would then shine for many days followed by other days of darkness. Instruments show that the day has probably lengthened several seconds since the beginning of written history. That seems but an atom of time. But that atom is always growing, for the pull of sun and moon never stops.

Both pictures may alarm us. But the past went long ago, and the future is still far off. For hundreds of thousands of years there will be no great change. Meanwhile, we can understand better how important the tides have been and will be in the life story of the earth on which we live.

Great Rivers of the Sea

The world's greatest rivers are in the sea. Beside them the Mississippi or even the Amazon is like a meadow brook. It seems odd that streams of water can move so far through other water without mixing. But a stream warmer or colder than the water all around it will flow on by itself for a long time. Sometimes its "banks" are almost as clearly marked as they would be on land. The Coast Guard steamer *Tampa* once paused on the edge of one of these strange sea rivers to take the temperature of the water. From the bow of the ship this was fifty-six degrees. From the stern it was only thirty-four.

The moving current may also differ in color from the surrounding sea. And sometimes its surface is choppy, or fogs may cover it.

The most important of these sea rivers is the Gulf Stream. It flows out of the Gulf of Mexico between Cuba and Florida. There it moves at a speed of about three miles an hour or as fast as we would care to walk. It is ninety miles wide and in places more than half a mile deep. Nearly two billion tons of water sweep along the Florida shore every minute.

The Gulf Stream moves along the Atlantic coast of the United States. Then past Cape Cod in Massachusetts, it curves eastward and sweeps on across the Atlantic. There it broadens out, slows down and loses much of the warmth it brought from tropic seas.

Now it divides into great branches. One of these washes the coasts of Iceland, another the shores of Great Britain and Norway where it pushes back the polar ice fields.

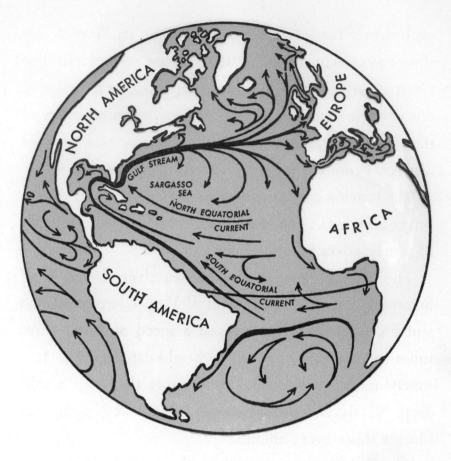

Arrows mark the great ocean rivers in the Atlantic.

And still another big branch curves south along the shores of Africa.

On land, rivers rise in some spring or pond and empty into a larger river or a lake or perhaps the ocean. You can tell on the map where they begin and end. But the great rivers of the sea have neither a beginning nor an end. Even

42

There are great rivers in the Pacific Ocean, too.

the mighty Gulf Stream is but a part of a larger system.

These rivers flow as they do because of three forces which are working upon them all the time. One of these is the spinning of the earth upon its axis. Another is the uneven heating of air and water by the sun. A third force is the continents and islands which break up these rivers just as rocks and sand bars break up a meadow brook.

The earth we know turns completely around every twenty-four hours. As the distance around it at the equator is about 24,000 miles and there are twenty-four hours in a day, the surface rocks are traveling at the rate of 1,000 miles an hour. They do not change position, but the air is so much lighter that it cannot quite keep up with them. And so we have those movements of the air that we call winds.

Where most of us live, winds change their direction often for many reasons. But on both sides of the equator where the earth spin is greatest they blow pretty constantly from one direction. They are called trade winds because in old times they bore sailing ships great distances.

Since the earth spins toward the east these trade winds come from the east. But the bulge of the earth at the equator swerves them a little from their course. North of the equator they swing to the right and blow from the northeast. South of the equator they swing to the left and blow from the southeast. Such steady winds drag the surface waters after them from east to west in what are called the equatorial currents.

The north equatorial current crosses the Atlantic and swings into the Gulf of Mexico. There the press of waters raises the level of the sea some inches higher than the open Atlantic to form the Gulf Stream. So at first the Gulf Stream is actually flowing downhill. After it has crossed the Atlantic, much of its waters turn south along the African coast to join the equatorial current.

And here we see how the continents change the direction of such ocean rivers. If it were not for Central America, the equatorial current would keep on across the Pacific. But it is forced northward by the continent of North America and so bends back upon itself in its endless course.

Where it flows from tropic seas, the Gulf Stream is warm water. It keeps much of this warmth as it crosses the Atlantic.

South of the equator there is a similar movement of waters although not quite so clearly marked. There are great rivers in the Pacific, too. In fact, another north equatorial current which crosses that ocean is 9,000 miles long.

This curves northward along the shores of the Philippines and other islands to recross the ocean as the Japanese Current. Although the Pacific is very large, its many islands break up the currents so that they are not so well marked as in the North Atlantic.

In the Indian Ocean, which is confined by the conti-

The flying fish uses his fins like the wings of an airplane.

nents of Africa and Asia and Australia, the currents do not have the same room in which to move about. And so they may change their direction from one season of the year to the other with the prevailing winds.

Sometimes ocean currents broaden out into drifts which may move scarcely a mile an hour. In other places they are held within narrow bounds by the land. Then they may speed up to ten miles or more. So the surface of the seas is crisscrossed by great rivers. Some are warm water; some cold moving endlessly about. There are also great areas where there is little movement. They are like eddies along a brook where the water seems to draw apart from the main stream for a rest.

There are other movements in the sea even greater than

the surface currents. These are the rising of warmer, lighter waters and the sinking of heavier, colder waters. The cold waters from the Polar Seas sink down to creep along the ocean floor, and the warm waters of the tropics press slowly over the surface toward the poles.

Such movements support all life within the sea. They bear life-giving oxygen down to the very ocean floor. They scatter about the salts and other minerals in the water just as farmers fertilize their fields. These minerals keep up the plant life which feeds the animal life of the sea.

At some seasons of the year the Gulf Stream is pushed southward a little by the cold Labrador Current. But most of the great rivers of the sea change their course very little. Scientists think that the Gulf Stream has been flowing for about 60 million years. But before Central America rose out of the sea to join the two continents, it swept on across the Pacific to the far-off shores of Asia.

All this is very wonderful. It is like the flow of blood in your veins from your heart to your finger tips and back over and over again. Doctors call this circulation. Life upon this earth depends quite as much upon the circulation of the sea as your own life depends upon the circulation of blood in your body.

All About the Sea

The surface currents, the rise and fall of waters, and the slow creep along the ocean floor cleanse and purify the sea. They keep it from becoming stagnant as you may have seen some stagnant pond all covered with green scum. There are a few places in the ocean like the deeper waters of the Black Sea where there is no circulation. Poisonous substances have gathered so that fish can no longer live there.

Scientists have figured that the waters of the Arctic Ocean are changed every 165 years like the water in a swimming pool. This is going on everywhere in the oceans and in most of the bays and inlets also. So when you stand upon the seashore, the waves that break at your feet may once have washed some coral island in the South Pacific or the frozen coasts of Greenland.

How the Sea Became Salty

If you have ever bathed in the sea and your mouth filled with water, I am sure you did not like it. And if it got in your eyes, it made them smart. For the water was unpleasantly salty.

Just how salty is the sea? It has salt enough to cover the whole United States to the depth of a mile and a half.

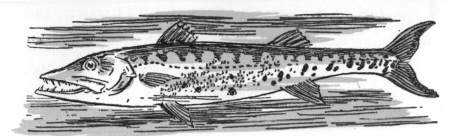

The great barracuda may be six to eight feet long.

Then all the mountains east of the Rockies would be buried in salt. Or if we put it another way, there is enough to make a continent of salt as big as Africa.

Not all the seas are equally salty. The amount varies a little from the surface to the bottom and from pole to pole. But the average is about three and one-half parts of salt for every hundred parts of water. The Atlantic, just north and south of the equator, is a bit saltier than the other oceans.

We find much greater differences among the smaller seas. The Red Sea, which stretches between the hot deserts of Arabia and Africa, is the saltiest of all. The Baltic Sea in Europe is the least so. The Red Sea is about six times as salty as the Baltic.

Much of the salt in the oceans seems to be mere waste. The life in the sea uses little of it, and so salt collects over the passing ages from the rivers which wash it down from the uplands. But a little finds its way back again. From the spray which the waves cast up along the shore, the winds carry tiny salt crystals for long distances. Many plants and trees which do not like salt do not grow well near the sea. Others seem to thrive on salt. Among these are asparagus and wild roses. Natives in the Far East think the clove tree is never happy unless it can hear the wash of the surf.

In some places the winds carry a great deal of salt far inland. In India there is a lake called Sambhar. Although it is 400 miles from the ocean, the winds each year scatter

The thresher shark may have a tail as long as his body.

3,000 tons of salt over the surface of this lake. And there are dry lake beds in Australia where the salt seems to be restored as fast as it is taken away by just such winds blowing from the sea.

In Utah there is a small "inland sea" called Great Salt Lake. It covers about 1,800 miles and contains water almost six times as salty as the ocean. Every year some 40,000 tons of salt are taken from this lake.

About three-quarters of the mineral matter in the sea is the same as the table salt which you sprinkle on your potatoes. But more than half of all the elements that make up matter have also been discovered there. Iron is found in the sea, and copper and even gold. In fact, there is gold enough to make every person in the world a millionaire. Men have been able to get a little of this gold from the sea. But so much water must be treated that the amount recovered does not pay for the expense.

Just how so much salt got into the sea is a problem which scientists are still trying to solve. The clouds which are always rising from the sea are fresh water. They leave the salt behind. If, as many scientists believe, the oceans once floated in clouds above the hot earth, those clouds held fresh water. As this rained down to fill the seas, much mineral matter must have been dissolved from the rocks.

And in the long ages that have passed, the rivers have been carrying more mineral matter from the uplands.

You will remember that other scientists believe that the seas slowly filled from water formed in the rocks deep down in the earth. Such water has been rising ever since. And it contains mineral matter. Even deep wells yield so much of this mineral that their waters are called "hard," and sometimes are unfit to drink.

We do not know how much salt was first dissolved from the rocks or how much has been added by the rivers or by steam rising from hot springs or volcanoes. For the salt in the sea is one of the most wonderful things in this wonderful world of ours. And like so many other wonderful things, it is a good deal of a mystery.

Life in the Sea

The First Life in the World

Once there was no life on the earth—no animal and no plant of any kind. All was dead matter. It may surprise you to know that the first life began in the sea.

Just how the first faint spark of that life was lighted in dead matter we do not know. But we do know that the sea had slowly collected all the elements that life requires. In some shallow bay or cove when sun and heat were exactly right, life stirred among these elements.

You may be told that the beginning of life was the Act of God. For all agree that some great power does control everything from the smallest to the greatest—from the atom to the star.

Even now we can see the elements combine into those strange things called *viruses*. They are so tiny that only through the most powerful microscope can we see them at all. And scientists wonder whether they are really alive or are mere specks of matter that are getting ready to live. Viruses may cause diseases such as scarlet fever and pneumonia. Some of them injure plants. Many seem harmless. We are just beginning to learn something about them.

Other tiny things are certainly alive. They are much larger than the viruses. Yet some of them are still so small that thousands placed side by side would not measure an inch. Some are the tiniest of plants; some the smallest of animals. There are others which may be called either plant or animal, as though Nature had not made up her mind which way to turn.

The smallest of these living things divide, and the halves divide again. So the divisions continue until from a single cell a great number form like a swarm of bees. For a long time all living things had but a single cell. Then after ages had passed, some cells, instead of scattering about, combined to form a larger plant or animal. Then step by step rose ever higher forms. And last of all came man, whose body is made up of millions upon millions of cells.

We can picture all this as a ladder up which life has slowly climbed. The tiny one-celled things managed to reach the first round of that ladder. Larger creatures climbed higher. Man has climbed highest of all and is still climbing.

Living things had swum the seas for many ages before they ventured out upon the shore. The slowly rising continents were barren rock and soil. Nothing grew on mountain slopes or in the valleys. The land was one great desert. All life was in the sea. This continued for tens of millions of years.

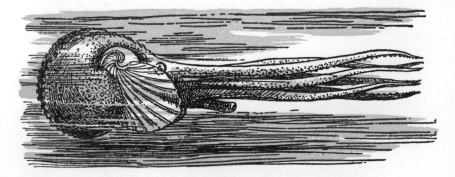

The shell of the paper nautilus is very lovely.

But as time went on, living things swam up the rivers and became accustomed to fresh water. In the mud of stream and swamp they found a new home. Then at last some of them crawled from the world of water out into the world of fresh air and sunlight.

And when, you ask, did life begin? We can read something of that story in the rocks. The remains of plants or creatures that we can study are found in rocks half a billion years old. They are all forms of sea life that had not yet appeared upon the land. But living things had already been swarming in the sea for a long time. We find traces of them in much older rocks that go back at least a billion years. These traces were of just such tiny creatures as still form the carpets of ooze on so much of the ocean floor. No doubt they rose from still older forms which once lived and passed away and have left no trace.

And there are other ways through which we learn something of the debt we owe the sea. Your very blood is salty. Now salt seems rather a useless thing. It plays but a small part in flesh and bone, but it seems needed in the blood. When you perspire on a hot day your body loses some of its salt. If this happens too suddenly, you may suffer.

Your blood holds about the same proportion of salt that

sea water held when the first living things with blood in their veins swam the sea. That salt is a reminder of the time, long ago, when creatures much farther down the scale of life commenced their upward climb. It is a reminder that you owe your origin to the sea, the mother of all life.

Yes, life not only began in the sea, but the sea sustains all life today. It is the source of moisture which every living thing requires. Even the cactus in the desert, though it can get along with very little, needs some moisture or it would die. If the seas dried up, the continents would dry up also and all life would disappear.

If we want to see what would happen then, we may look at the moon. The moon has no sea, no water and no life. It is a dead world.

The sea not only gave birth to life, but watches over all life today. For without her generous waters, no life could long survive.

Sea Meadows and Sea Gardens

Perhaps you have walked in a meadow on a warm summer day. The grass was like a green carpet dotted with yellow buttercups and white daisies. How beautiful it was—how full of life!

The chambered nautilus has a house of many rooms.

Or you may have seen those sandy wastes that we call deserts. Perhaps a few withered plants were struggling to keep alive in the hot sun. But still the landscape seemed empty, as though it were dying, if not already dead.

The sea also has its meadows and its deserts. True, sea meadows are quite diffcrent from those we find in Vermont or Wisconsin. Their plants are far more numerous. But because they are so small you might sail among them and never know that life was all about you.

Scientists like to explore these meadows of the sea. Like fishermen, they use a net. Only their net is of woven silk. With this net trailing behind a moving boat, they skim the waters for some of the tiny plants and animals that swarm there. These are called *plankton* which, to the old Greeks, meant *wandering*. The name is well chosen for plankton are carried about by winds, tides and currents.

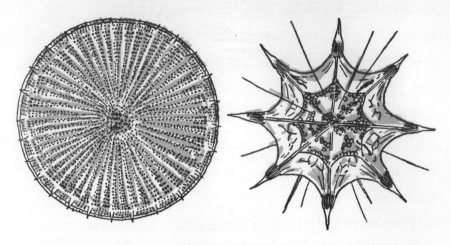

A diatom (left) and radiolarian are tiny as a speck of dust.

The most useful of the plant life that this silken net skims from the waves are called *diatoms*. If you could place one of the largest of these on clear glass, it would be like a speck of dust. Diatoms are unbelievably tiny. They are so small that a quart of water drawn from the Kiel Canal in Germany contained more than six million diatoms.

With a microscope we can make these tiny plants appear larger. In this way we can study them and learn more about them.

Actually diatoms are of many shapes and sizes. Each one is enclosed in a tiny glass case marked with beautiful designs. Diatoms seem almost like fairy dishes but are very much alive. In Polar Seas they swarm in such numbers that they color the water a glassy green. If you could rub some of this water between your fingers, you could get the gritty feel of the diatoms.

Diatoms are true plants and form the food of many small sea animals and fish. Sometimes they grow in yellow patches on the under belly of the great blue whale called the *sulphur bottom*.

Even lovelier are other tiny plants with a long name— *radiolarians*. Like the diatoms, they also live in glass houses. But these are even more richly ornamented. They bristle with spikes and spines. They glitter like gems. But no jeweler ever designed anything half so fine.

These meadows of the sea flourish in the spring just as the grass and flowers do in upland fields. They also wither in the summer sun.

Just as upland fields have their bees and ants and dragon flies, so the meadows of the sea have much animal life. Most important are tiny shrimp-like creatures called *copepods*. They usually make up two-thirds of the yield of a plankton net. One of these copepods may swallow no fewer than 120,000 diatoms in a single day.

And as they eat, they too are eaten. For more than 60,000 copepods have been taken from the stomach of a single herring. Both fish and whales eat them. They swim along the surface with their mouths wide open, then strain the copepods through ribbons of whale bone that hang from their upper jaws like whiskers. Whalers call these copepods *brit*.

In the Polar Seas where copepods are so numerous, they sometimes color the water as though with floating brick dust. More than 300 gallons of "copepod soup" have been taken from the stomach of a great blue whale.

Such is the life that swarms in the meadows of the sea. But there are other even stranger creatures. Some have big heads and horns and staring eyes. Some give off light like fireflies. A ship passing through them at night seems to stir a trail of smouldering fire.

Then, too, there are the eggs of fish and baby clams and oysters and lobsters which float for a while until they settle down upon the bottom.

Most tiny floating plants are useful, but a few are dangerous. One species along Pacific shores forms reddish streaks in the water and glows at night with a pale green light. Fish and shellfish that eat these plants might poison us if we ate them.

Just as the uplands have their deserts as well as their meadows, so has the sea. There are waste spaces where plant and animal life are scarce. Much of Hudson Bay is poorly supplied and so are great regions of the open sea.

Less important than the tiny plants that float upon the surface are those other plants that grow along the shores. They are called seaweeds, which isn't a very good name. For a weed is one of those harmful or useless plants in our garden. Seaweeds are merely the larger plant life of the sea.

Upland plants are almost always green. That is because of the wonder substance *chlorophyl* in their leaves. With this substance and the sunbeams, the leaves make sugar, starch and even wood mainly out of air and water.

Some seaweeds are green such as the sea lettuce and other algae. Some are blue green. And many are red. But the larger plants are olive green or brown.

They grow only in shallow waters where the light soon fades. Below a certain depth they cannot grow at all. For all plants, except a few like mushrooms, need the sun.

Unlike land plants, seaweeds have no roots, and few have blossoms. They get all their food from the water, none from the soil. Many cling to rocks, but that is merely to keep from being washed about by the waves. The giant kelp of the Pacific has great floating leaves, and its stems may be 200 feet long. It grows in beds all the way to

All About the Sea

Alaska. No African jungle swarms with so much wild life as these strange jungles of the sea.

One kind of giant kelp grows off the shores of the Aleutian Islands. It holds fast to the ocean floor by a stem so tough that Eskimos once used it for fish lines. From a central floating bladder, rubbery leaves spread out like a big blossom fifty feet across. This strange plant is called sea otter cabbage. For the sea otter which swims about for fish climbs upon that floating bladder. There he loves to doze as though in a cradle rocked by the ocean swells.

Many other seaweeds have air-filled spaces which act as floats. Some break loose from the rocks and drift far from shore. Sometimes they gather where the surface is not disturbed by the great rivers of the sea.

The strangest of all these lonely places stretches across the Atlantic from near the Azore Islands toward Bermuda. It covers an area two-thirds as large as the United States. It is called the Sargasso Sea because of a kind of seaweed called *sargassum*. This seaweed has collected in floating fields sometimes several feet in thickness with broad lanes of water in between.

Many weird stories have been told about the Sargasso Sea. In the early days it was thought that sailing ships might be caught there and never get away. But we now know that they can sail through such weedy waters. Even

Columbus crossed a part of the Sargasso Sea and wondered at the queer life he found there. For tiny crabs crawl about and odd fish hide in the weed.

As in the upland meadows much of the plant life of the sea has its seasons. And as it flourishes, so does the animal life that feeds upon it. One February a plankton net skimmed 400 copepods from the waters of the North Sea. Two months later it caught four million.

Giant kelp (left) and sea palm grow on the ocean floor.

If you visit the seashore in the fall, you will find the beach strewn with larger seaweeds. There will be great heaps of rubbery kelp and rock weed. And the sands may be marked like red ink with the red algae which have washed ashore and dried in the sun. That is what fishermen call the harvest of the sea.

Some of the loveliest of all gardens are also in the sea. They are found in tropic climates where the water is warm. But strange to say, life in those gardens is less plant

Corals grow in many forms and colors.

than animal. We find sponges of many shapes and hues and brilliant sea anemones. Queer sea fans and rainbow fish swim about.

Most wonderful of all are the corals. These tiny animals leave a limey skeleton when they die. Some of these form precious corals so beautiful that they are made into jewelry. Others collect in great masses.

Many islands in the South Pacific are the work of these coral animals. They even built the Great Barrier Reef which stretches for more than 800 miles along the coast of Australia. Florida rests upon coral rock and sand. More than any other living creature except man himself, the corals have changed the surface of the earth.

The Kingdom of the Tides

Along the seashore for several hours each day we find a strange new world opening up before us. This is the strip of ocean floor laid bare when the sea falls back from the land at ebb tide. Then sand bars appear like islands, or deep pools hide among the rocks. There we are likely to meet some of the strange creatures that live in the sea.

Many of them are busy, active workers. They dig tunnels and plant gardens and build houses and even cities.

All About the Sea

Among them are carpenters and masons and boat builders and weavers. We must confess there are burglars, too, with fine sets of burglar tools. These are the "little people" of the sea. The country they live in has well been called the Kingdom of the Tides.

Suppose we go exploring this kingdom on a summer day along New England coasts. Far off beyond the outer sands or rocks, the waves are playing. The friendly sea has slipped back as if to say, "You are welcome. Only hurry, for I am coming back again."

We shall need to take a small shovel to dig with and a pail for some of the treasures we may find. We would be wise to carry a small magnifying glass, too. For some of the little creatures and their works are very, very small.

First let us roam across this sand bar. A few hours ago it was covered with water. Now at ebb tide, the water has slipped back. The sand bar points at the sea like a long finger.

Its surface is marked with ridges where the waves have heaped the sand. And there are tiny rivers that carry off the water that was left behind. They wash deep trenches in the sand, just as much larger rivers would do inland.

Look at that jet of water spurting up like a small geyser. Dig quickly if you would find what makes it. He is trying to get away, and the only way he can go is down. Now you have him! Pull, and pull hard! He seems to have roots as he holds fast to the sands. But here he comes with his two long shells like an old-time razor. He is called a razor clam and very tasty is his creamy white flesh.

And what is that other hole beside your foot? "Only a worm," you say. But do not draw away, for the worms are a big family among the creatures of the sea. There are many, many kinds. Some are beautiful, and all are interesting.

This one is called a clam worm, for he eats clams. But fish eat him, and fishermen use him to bait their hooks.

See that odd tube sticking out of the sand. It is made of bits of shell and seaweed glued together. Another kind of worm has made it, and he thinks it is a comfortable home.

Here is a bit of driftwood that the tide has left. Why, it is as full of holes as a honeycomb! You can break it in your fingers. Then you will see each hole is lined to look like the finest china.

The boring clam or *teredo* has dug those tunnels for a home. He is an expert carpenter. He has lined the rooms with plaster finer and smoother than any builder could do. But he has done much damage, too, although he didn't mean to. For he has, in times past, injured the bottoms of wooden ships so that they sank at sea.

What strange thing is this? For all the world, he looks like a little green hedgehog. He is covered with green spines and is called a sea urchin. Turn him over and see his mouth with five sharp teeth that meet at a point. His shell is made up of thousands of plates that fit together. By moving his spines he can crawl slowly over the sand. The sea urchin is thought to be a mason also. For on some rocky coasts he seems to drill holes in the very rock as shelters from the waves.

Here is a lovely sea star with five purple fingers. Each finger is grooved and filled with tiny tubes that writhe and twist. If you should cut him into five equal parts and throw him into the sea, each arm could grow into a new starfish.

And what is this odd creature crawling in from the shallow water? He looks like a big spider and indeed is called a spider crab. Notice the seaweed growing on his back. He has planted it there so hungry fish will not see him when he hides on the bottom. The spider crab is an expert gardener. He has a big cousin who lives in deep waters off Japan. That one has legs that can spread ten feet or more.

On the beach you see a sea star and spider crab (in back)
and a horseshoe crab and sea urchin (in front).

All About the Sea

What is this moving toward us like an armored tank? His body is shaped something like a horse's foot, so he is called a horseshoe crab. But he isn't really a crab at all. He has a long, slim tail with which he can right himself when you turn him on his back. See how closely his jointed legs come together. He has no teeth so he chews his food between his knees or elbows. He likes the fat worms of the tide flats. He can see fairly well, for he has several eyes.

The horseshoe crab comes from a family that goes back for hundreds of millions of years. His ancestors once ruled the world long before the dinosaurs. So let him go his way and do not hurt him as some thoughtless people do.

And what is the yellow plant growing all over this oyster shell? It isn't a plant but an animal—the boring sponge. Pick up the shell and see how it falls to pieces in your fingers. The sponge has eaten it full of holes. He can eat holes in cement blocks on piers or breakwaters.

And here is a different kind of sponge that looks like a glove. It is called a finger sponge. In warmer seas, sponges sometimes grow to a great size. For thousands of years divers have gathered them.

Here is a patch of mud. Scrape some up, and look at it through your magnifying glass. Why it seems alive, and it is. Several kinds of shrimplike creatures make their homes in the soft mud. If your magnifying glass were stronger, you could see some wonderful gardens of diatoms, those tiny plants which float in such numbers in the sea. They also grow even better in the mud.

Now we come to one of the cities in the sea. "What," you say, "only a bed of mussels!" True, but there must be thousands of them—enough surely to make a city. Each mussel has spun strong, tough threads to hold him in place, for he is an expert weaver. In Italy these threads

A sea turtle comes out of the water to lay her eggs.

are woven into gloves. In France and other countries mussels are prized for food. Most Americans do not seem to know they are good to eat.

Here we come to a big rock and another kind of city. "Only barnacles!" True, but every one of them has built a house upon the rock. Each house has walls. While it has no windows, its roof can be moved. Through this roof, the barnacle inside sends out soft feelers that look like tiny ostrich plumes. With these he gathers the floating plants which are his food. His cities have many thousands of dwellings.

In Australia barnacles grow several inches high. And people eat them, for they are relatives of the shrimps, although you would never guess it.

Most barnacles do not like to travel. But the whale barnacles fasten their homes to the bodies of whales. In that way they get a free ride for thousands of miles.

And here is a shell like an upturned boat. The creature which lived inside once clung to a rock. The shell has a half deck and can float quite well in this tiny pool.

And here is another kind of shell about an inch in length. How beautiful it is with its spiral shape! But oystermen would not agree, for this is the oyster drill

The white bear of the Arctic seems at home in the waves.

that kills so many young oysters. Within that shell, curled like the spring of a watch, he carries a tongue covered with teeth like a file. With this he drills a hole through the shell that the oyster has made as a house. What a robber he turned out to be!

There the little drill has sunk to the bottom among a cluster of bright flowers. These are sea anemones. Although they are animals, not plants, they are often called the blossoms of the sea. Sea anemones have fringed edges which are always moving. As they move, they feed upon tiny water plants that are so small you cannot see them.

And what is this odd thing splashing in the shallow water? He is called a *squid*. The tide has ebbed, and he is worried. What a queer head he has with its big eyes!

75

All About the Sea

And those arms or feelers that twist about as he seeks a way into deeper water! Each arm has cuplike suckers on the under side with which he can grasp a small fish. And he has a beak, like a bird's, to bite with.

His body, about eight inches long, is a pale brick red and shaped like a torpedo. In fact, the squid is sometimes called the Torpedo of the Sea because he can dart about very quickly.

You would never guess how unless you saw him do it. He fills his mouth with water, then spits it out so quickly that it pushes him backward, tail first. Just touch him with the shovel and see what he will do. Why, he spits out something black as ink! He does this to cloud the water so that he can escape from his enemies. It is ink and has long been used as such in Mediterranean countries.

Now look away out there. The tide is turning, and the waves are rolling in, edged with white foam. The sea is coming back, and the sea creatures all about us are happy now. They would rather hide beneath the friendly waves than be left where you can find them. Under the waves they can begin their digging and building, their weaving and planting.

We must go now. In some parts of the world we would have to hurry, for there the tide comes in as fast as a man

Globe fish.   Cornet fish.   Sole.

can run. In New England the tide comes in slowly so we have plenty of time.

And tomorrow we can come again. For we might spend many an afternoon, yes, and a whole lifetime, getting better acquainted with the little creatures who live in the Kingdom of the Tides.

Down Where All Is Cold and Dark

The strangest of all strange regions in the sea is neither near the surface nor upon the ocean floor. It lies somewhere in between. There is no sky above nor ground beneath but water everywhere. No creature that lives there has a home like the clam in the mud or the barnacle upon a rock. There is no place where he can go to escape his enemies. He is always moving about.

Only three men have ever seen this strange world down there so far beneath the waves. Off the island of Bermuda, Dr. Beebe and a helper were let down 3,028 feet into the sea. They traveled in a hollow steel globe. That was in 1934. In 1949 off the coast of California Otis Barton went down about 4,500 feet. Through thick glass windows these men sent light rays out into the dark waters. And through those windows, strange creatures that no

In a hollow steel globe Dr. Beebe went far below the waves.

one had ever seen before peered in at the men from land.

What would we find if we, too, could dive so far below the surface? First of all, we would notice that the light grows dim, then fades altogether. Hold up a glass of water and you can see through it easily. But you could not see through a mile of water or even 200 feet.

As you go down in your iron globe with thick glass windows, you would find that the sunbeams do not reach very far below the surface. Red light soon fades, then yellow, and then green. Down about 150 feet only blue light remains. There everything would seem blue as though you were wearing blue glasses.

And you would see nothing clearly but as though through a mist or fog. Dr. Beebe could barely read a printed page at a depth of about 400 feet. At 1,900 feet, the last dim ray of blue light went out and all was dark.

It is very cold so far below the surface of the water. At the equator, surface waters may have a temperature of 82 degrees. Six hundred feet down they are 30 degrees colder. In most places in the sea, the temperature drops all the way to the ocean floor. There it falls below the freezing point. But it cannot freeze, for reasons that we shall see a little later.

This in-between region of the sea is a strange world. It is so dark and chill with nothing underneath except a mile or more of still colder waters. Yet there is much life in this area. It is unlike any found elsewhere on land or sea.

If we search for plants, we find none. For plants need sunlight and warmth. Neither the diatoms that swarm in such numbers on surface waters nor the larger plants that float in the Sargasso Sea could live in those sunless depths. Only animal life gropes about in the darkness and the cold.

What do they eat, those strange and always hungry creatures? All food comes to them from above. Dead plants and fish and other life in surface waters sink slowly down to them. And failing this, they eat one another. For "eat or be eaten" is the only law in their lawless world.

And what kind of life would we find there? Sea jellies of many shapes and colors would go drifting by. Some would wave like ribbons. Some would trail long feelers. Arrow worms would swim past in troops. Queer things with wing-like shells called *pteropods* would dart about like dragon flies.

Most abundant of all are shrimplike creatures. Some are transparent like a pane of glass. Some are highly colored. They swarm like insects of the deep seas.

The fish would startle and perhaps scare you. Some have teeth so long that they can never close their mouths. One kind has a stomach that can stretch so much that he can swallow a fish three times larger than himself. They have been given queer names: the Black Gulper, the Swallower, the Sea Viper, and the Dragon Fish. One known as the Angler carries a bony rod on his head bearing a stout line and three hooks.

Some creatures in this weird world have great staring

eyes. Others have no eyes at all. The most common body colors are black and red. And new kinds, never seen before, are being brought up from time to time by ships dredging in deep waters.

How do they see to get about down there where sunlight never comes? That is one of the wonders of this watery world. What little light there is, is the kind that the fireflies used on summer nights. It has been called cold light, for it gives off little or no heat. Scientists know it as *phosphorescence*. They have studied it, but unlike the strange shrimps and fish, they have not learned how to make it.

We have the same kind of light on the surface of the sea. There much of it comes from certain bacteria which are among the smallest of all the plants. These have been called the tiniest lamps in creation. A few fish even take groups of these bacteria into their own bodies to light their way about at night.

But in the depths, where it is always dark, fish may have a row of bright spots along each side which look like the portholes of a passenger steamer. Some can turn these lights on or off just as you can a flashlight.

This light is mostly white. But it may be red, green, yellow, blue or even purple. One fish carries red lights

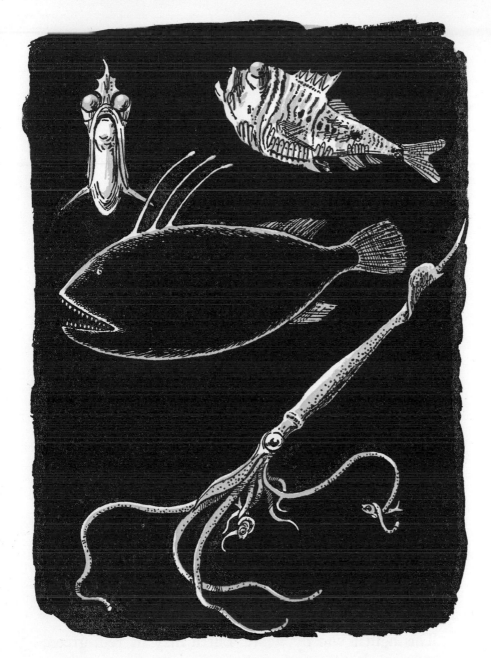

Silver hatchet (top right); angler (center); and sea squid.

on his head and blue lights near his tail. A squid, which is sometimes found two miles below the surface, flashes red, white and blue.

But you ask, "Why do these queer creatures stay where they are?" That is a fair question. Life in the sea is largely controlled by temperature and pressure. The temperature declines, and the pressure grows greater the deeper we go. The creatures down there would not be happy in the warmer waters at the surface. Nor does anything lead them to explore the deeper waters below.

Some fish are held captive by their swimming bladders. This is a sack filled with air. It helps the fish to move easily about. It acts something like the rubber ring that you may have clung to when you were learning to swim.

Greater pressures keep the fish from going deeper. If he ventures too far in the other direction, the pressure may push him to the surface. Then he really "falls upward." And so he "stays put" in this dark, cold space with no boundaries anywhere.

Strange Life in the Ocean Deeps

Life in that watery world where there is no top nor bottom seems strange enough. But how about the greater depths below? Fully one half the sea is three miles deep or more. Can anything live down there on the basement floor of the world?

For a long time this great area was thought to be a desert as dead as outer space. First of all there was the pressure of the water. Pearl divers in the South Pacific go down 100 feet. A man in a diving suit can go down for about 500. Beyond that only a steel globe like Dr. Beebe's can stand a pressure that would crush a house like an eggshell. A mile below the surface that pressure is about a ton for every square inch of surface. In the deepest troughs of the Pacific it is seven tons.

Even the water itself yields to such pressure. Fill a bottle, and it will hold no more. For water, though soft and yielding, cannot be crowded into a smaller space. But that is not true of the deep sea. Place one brick upon another, and the brick beneath will remain firm. But if we piled 10,000 bricks upon it something might happen. Pile water drop upon drop not for inches or for feet but for miles, and the drops at the bottom are squeezed more and more. If the very sea did not yield to such pressure, it would rise everywhere about ninety feet. Then every seaport in the world would be flooded, many islands would disappear, and great areas of the continents would

Floating icebergs are sometimes nearly 300 feet high.

be buried beneath the waves rolling in from all sides.

There is another curious thing about water. Most things swell with heat and shrink with cold. So does water—up to a certain point. It shrinks with falling temperatures until just before it freezes. Then it begins to swell. Ice, as you know, floats to the surface because it is so much lighter than the water. Even icebergs hundreds of feet high go drifting across the sea. If this were not so, the Polar Seas might freeze clear to the bottom. Then the whole world would be slowly chilled, and all living things might die.

Fresh water freezes when the thermometer goes down to 32 degrees above zero. Salt water will stand a few more degrees of cold. And the great pressure also helps to prevent freezing. So in the sea we find temperatures near 27 degrees. The deep sea does not freeze. But even so, how could life endure such constant cold?

Besides, men thought there could be no air at such depths and all life needs oxygen. Nor was there anything to eat. Clearly there was no life upon the ocean floor because there couldn't be.

But in spite of all these things that seem to make life impossible, some creatures do live down there. We are just beginning to learn something about them. A squid has been brought up from a depth of more than three miles. A queer fish has been caught some 20,000 feet below the surface or nearly four miles. Strange creatures called sea spiders, a kind of crab, crawl about. Sea worms have been dredged up from their snug burrows on the ocean floor.

The darkness does not bother them, for they have never known the light. Nor does the cold, for their bodies have much the same temperature. Nor does the pressure, for they were born there and have always been used to it. True there is little oxygen but enough for their small needs. For the waters of the Polar Seas, which carry some air, sink to the bottom and creep along the ocean floor.

Food is a problem. Life depends upon bits of dead plants or animals that rain slowly down from above. This is food that got by the black gulpers and the dragon fish and those other dwellers in the watery world above.

Cameras have been lowered into these deeps which have never known the light since the seas began. Flashlight pictures have been taken of sea spiders. Some day, no doubt, we shall have many more and better pictures.

The black gulper lives down where all is cold and dark.

The sea provides more room for life than the uplands do. There all creatures live on or near the ground. Earthworms burrow a bit, and so do moles and ground hogs. Birds fly up into the trees, and monkeys swing from the branches. Yet almost all land life is found within a hundred feet of the surface.

But the sea with nearly three times as much surface as the land can support life down to its deepest depths. It has more than 300 times as much space for living things as do all the continents and islands.

Bright Carpets on the Ocean Floor

Life in the sea does not lose interest for us when that life has passed away. For there all dead and forgotten things keep on collecting. We carry old chairs and pictures and dishes into our basement to gather dust from year to year. Then some day that basement is cleaned out, and things are put in order. The ocean floor is the great basement of the world. But it can never be cleaned out or the dust removed. And so time working through long ages weaves dust and all the other rubbish of the sea into the largest and most wonderful carpets in the world.

What we call the dry land is always melting away. The

rocks crumble to make the soil in which things grow. The winds blow this soil about and grind it into dust. The rains wash it into the rivers, and the rivers carry it to the sea. Every year they bear away soil enough to make a mountain four miles long and a mile high.

Along the shallows that we call the continental shelves, such waste becomes mud. This mud is mixed with dead seaweed and animal matter. It is mainly of three colors— red, green and blue.

Red mud varies from red-brown to yellow-brown. It is common in the Yellow Sea, in China and along the coasts of Brazil.

Green mud is found along the Atlantic coast of North America, in Australia, South Africa and Japan.

Blue mud is much more abundant than the others. It isn't always blue, for it may be dull gray or brown and sometimes nearly black.

Such many-colored muds cover the continental shelves, and drape the steep slopes. But the ocean floor has other, stranger carpets.

These are of two kinds, the *oozes* and the *clays*. The oozes are not formed from the waste of the continents but from millions upon millions of tiny creatures that once swam in surface waters. Many had tiny shells like the clams and oysters. Dying, their shells rained down like snowflakes upon the bottom of the sea. There they form a sticky paste called by a long name, *globigerina ooze*.

Other tiny creatures dart about like white moths. They, too, have a long name, *pteropods*. And their shells also form a limey ooze.

In some places globigerina ooze accumulates quite rapidly. An inch or more may be laid down in ten years. It is found in patches in all the seas. It covers about two thirds of the Atlantic floor, perhaps half that of the Indian Ocean, and one third of the Pacific. There is enough to hide all the continents with millions of square miles left over. Its colors range from white to brown, but may be tinted rose, yellow, blue or green.

Tiny shells form a mud known as globigerina ooze.

This ooze hardens into chalk. The White Cliffs of Dover in England are of such chalk. It may harden still more into limestone and marble. Many tiny creatures once lived and died in the sea to make the piece of chalk with which you write upon the blackboard.

A smaller carpet is formed from the glassy shells of diatoms and other plants. Great bands of this ooze stretch across the Pacific. A broad belt north of Antarctica reaches clear around the world. There is enough of it to cover all of North America.

Globigerina and diatom ooze are the common ocean carpets down to a depth of two miles or more. But greater deeps have quite a different covering. It is called *clay*. It is found over great areas in the Atlantic and Indian Oceans, but it is the favorite choice of the Pacific. For perhaps three-fifths of that biggest of the oceans lies above vast beds of clay.

This clay puzzled scientists for a long time. Now they believe it was formed in much the same way as globigerina ooze. In those cold depths with the crushing pressure of the water, the lime has melted away. A few minerals are left such as iron, aluminum and manganese. With them is mixed the dust of shooting stars that burned out in the upper air. This dust from outer space has rained

The White Cliffs of Dover are chalk made from tiny shells.

down upon the ocean floor for millions of years and helped to give the black clay a reddish color.

How rapidly this clay accumulates no one knows. But it is doubtful if an inch of it would collect in 1,000 years. With this clay are mixed the teeth of great sharks that swam the seas millions of years ago, and there are the ear bones of whales. Those bones are so hard that they outlast any other part of the whale's great skeleton.

Scientists have studied these carpets. They drive a hollow tube into them much like an apple corer. Cores seventy feet long have been drawn up from the bottom of the sea. These show deposits that may have collected for thousands of years.

Some cores bring back layers of sand. These layers may be ten feet thick. But sand is formed by the waves that grind the rocks along the shore. How did it get so far from land? Perhaps it was carried by floating ice that melted and dumped it on the ocean floor. Perhaps—but no one knows.

For a long time scientists feared they would never be able to learn how thick these carpets are. But they are beginning to get some light. Sound travels to a distant object and bounces back again as an echo. Knowing how fast it travels we can tell how far off the object is.

Radar waves work on the same principle. Such waves have been sent to the moon and have bounced back to the earth again.

A bomb is exploded under water. The sound travels to the bottom of the sea. An echo comes back. And so we can tell how deep the sea is in any place. Sound waves can also be sent through carpets of ooze or clay until they rebound from the solid rock beneath.

A study of such waves shows that ocean carpets in some places are 12,000 feet thick or more than two miles!

From woodcut by Hokusai

On the Watery Trail of the Fish

It was about 300 million years ago that the first fish appeared in the sea. Strange creatures, they died out long ago. But they were the great-grandfathers of those we know today. Nature must have loved them, for of all animals with backbones they are the most numerous. Scientists have listed over 20,000 species. As life overflowed from the sea to the land, some of the fish found their way into streams and lakes. Others spent part of their time in the sea and part in fresh water. But three-fifths of all the species, and by far the greatest number of individuals, stayed in the sea.

We have learned something about the strange fish that lurk in the deep sea. But those which we know best and which find their way to our dinner tables do not live very far below the waves. They gather along the continental shelves. Some of them like warm water; others prefer cold. Let the temperature rise or fall even a few degrees, and they move on or die.

Fish also go where they can find the most food. The North Sea between the British Isles and Europe is a favorite feeding ground with its floating meadows of diatoms and copepods. Sea fish also like their water salty. When the Baltic grew too fresh, the herring left and the oysters died.

Ocean fish are of two kinds, the surface feeders and those which root like pigs in the mud and sand. The one kind eats the floating plankton. The other grubs for worms and shellfish along the bottom.

They dress in colors that fit their surroundings. For they wish to hide from their enemies. Thus the mackerel and the herring are blue or silvery like the dancing waves. They swim on or near the surface. The bottom feeders, like the cod or the flounder, prefer colors of gray or brown. Fish that live among coral reefs may have all the hues of the rainbow.

While some fish are less than an inch long, the great whale shark may exceed fifty feet.

The mackerel (top) and herring (center) are blue or silvery.
An angler (lower) is big enough to swallow seventy herring.

All About the Sea

Most fish are covered with scales which lap over one another like the shingles on a roof. A few have bony plates like the sturgeon. Some are protected by bony spikes. The shark has a hide as rough as sandpaper.

The tail and fins of fish are arranged in many different ways. The sunfish, which may weigh two tons, has no tail at all. The oarfish seems to be all tail. Though he is scarcely two inches thick, he may be thirty feet long. He flashes through the waves like a silvery ribbon. Norwegian fishermen call him the King of the Herring for no good reason. He has weak jaws or none at all. But the angler, or goose fish, seems to be half jaws. In muddy water they yawn like an open trap. He has been known to catch sea gulls or even foxes which were running over the tide flats. A single angler five feet long had swallowed seventy herring.

Most fish swim with their tails and steer with their fins. The big sailfish has a tall fin along his back which looks like the sail on a Chinese junk. The flying fish uses his fins like the wings of an airplane. Breaking out of a wave he can dart through the air for 200 feet or more. Sometimes he falls on the decks of ships at night bringing a free breakfast. For he is good eating. Some fish leave the water and climb up the roots of trees with their fins.

Most fish prey upon other or smaller fish. They chase them as a cat does a mouse. A few are armed with weapons which they use with great skill. The swordfish and the sawfish strike the water with their bony snouts, then eat the fish which they have stunned. The big manta does the same with his winglike fins. The thresher shark has a tail as long as his whole body. Its sharp bony edge cuts like a swinging scythe. The stingray carries a poisoned dagger in his tail. The torpedo fish stuns his prey with electric shocks.

The soles and sand dabs are so flat they look as though they had been stepped upon. The garfish, long and slender, really looks like a file. The globe fish huffs and puffs himself into a spiney ball.

There are giants among the common fish. The record halibut was about ten feet long and weighed over 700 pounds. A cod has been caught that weighed over 200 pounds.

Some fish live a long time. They have been kept in tanks for more than fifty years. Many fish bear a record of their age on each scale. It is ringed like the stump of a tree to show the years of growth.

Almost all fish lay eggs. A flounder may lay a million eggs, a cod nine million, a sunfish three hundred million.

All About the Sea

Very few of these eggs ever grow into fish. Some sharks and skates lay eggs several inches long. They are enclosed in cases that look like rubber. Old seafaring men call them "sailors' purses."

The trail of some fish is one of Nature's secrets that no one can explain. Salmon leave the sea to go back to the very fresh water stream in which they were born. They fight their way against the current, leaping over rocks and even up waterfalls. There may be so many of them that they fill the channel. Having reached the place they seek, they lay their eggs and die.

Just how they find the right stream or river is more wonderful than radio or television. They have no maps; they can see but little under water. There is no one to direct their course.

Still stranger is the trail of the eels. When English eels are perhaps eight years old, they leave the pond or stream they live in. They wriggle, like snakes, across the wet grass at night. Then reaching the seashore they swim across the Atlantic to the waters near Bermuda. There they dive far below the surface, lay their eggs and die. The baby eels are transparent as glass with two dots for eyes.

They swim to the surface then start on the long jour-

Salmon leap over rocks and even up waterfalls.

ney homeward. This journey may take them two or three years. Most of them die or are eaten. Those which live change shape and color.

How do they know where to go, when they have never traveled that route before? You can answer that question as well as the wisest scientists, for no one knows.

A few fish are enemies to man. The fierce barracuda of Florida reefs looks like a big pike. With his razor-sharp teeth he sometimes attacks swimmers. Even more feared are sharks. Most of them are harmless, but a few are called "man eaters." On many beaches nets are stretched on poles to protect bathers in the sea. A few fish also have poisonous fins or spines.

Sea fish are prized most of all as food. Here the herring is the most important. But useful also are the cod, haddock, mackerel, tuna, halibut, flounder, and many other species.

Some people like fishing for sport. But it is also a big industry. Millions of dollars are invested in fishing boats and nets and all the things that such boats need. And millions more are spent in drying or smoking or salting or freezing or canning fish for market.

For fish have played no small part in history. The Dutch and English wrangled for many years over fishing in the North Sea. This country and Great Britain had many arguments over the Grand Banks of Newfoundland and the halibut fisheries in the Pacific. Portuguese fishermen still cross the Atlantic for cod.

People of many nations—the Norwegians, the Japanese and others—depend upon fish for much of their food. But the ocean is very large and has more to offer than has ever been used.

In recent years we are learning something about deeper waters. Radar waves have come bouncing back from moving masses down below. It has been thought these might be dense clouds of plankton. But it seems more likely they may be schools of fish. If so, they may yet add much to our food supply. Then what seem like empty spaces in the sea may help to feed a hungry world.

Land Animals That Put to Sea

Along our seacoasts are many creatures that are not quite sure whether they prefer to live on land or in the sea. Some crabs leave the sea and return only at certain seasons of the year. Then they meet great sea turtles which weigh hundreds of pounds coming up out of the water to lay their eggs in the warm sands.

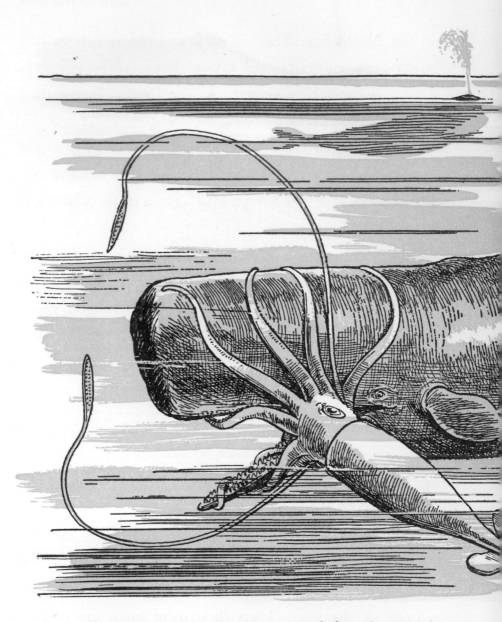

The giant squid battles the sperm whale with terrible arms.

The squid will be bitten and swallowed by the whale.

Most interesting are the whales and their many relatives. These great creatures were once much smaller land animals. For some reason they found the sea more attractive and returned there. Because the water bore up their weight, they grew larger and larger. Largest of all is the great blue whale which likes the lonely seas around Antarctica. That is because those cold waters are so rich in the diatoms and copepods which are his food.

He is the largest animal that has ever lived upon the earth. Even the dinosaurs that once went blundering about were small compared with him. One of these whales caught off the icy island of New Georgia was 107 feet long and weighed 125 tons.

There are several kinds of whales—the fin back, the hump back, the right whale, and others. The only large whale which has teeth is the sperm whale. Though he seldom reaches a length of seventy feet, he is the master of the seas. With his great lower jaw he can bite a large boat in two. He could also crush it with one blow of his tail. His head is so hard that he has been known to ram it through the side of a sailing ship. As he fears nothing, he is not so swift in his movements as the other whales. He feeds on giant squid, diving far down to get them in that cold, dark world in which they live.

Only a few giant squid have ever been found upon the surface of the sea. One of them was more than fifty feet long. His great eyes were nearly a foot across, for the light where he lives is very dim. His long arms had suckers as big as saucers rimmed with claws like tiger's claws. In battles with these monsters the whale's body is often scarred by those terrible arms. But the squid is no match for the sperm whale. He is soon bitten into pieces and swallowed. The sperm whale's only enemies were men who once hunted him for his oil.

More dreaded and savage is a smaller cousin called the *killer*. He grows to a length of thirty feet or more and is very stocky and powerful. He has large teeth in both jaws and is the terror of the seas. He swallows baby seals whole. While he lets the fighting sperm whale alone, a group of killers will attack other whales like a pack of wolves. They rip off the whale's big lips and tear out his tongue. The killer's tall back fin showing above the water is like a pirate's flag that warns of danger.

An odd member of the whale family is the narwhale of the Arctic. The male has a tooth which may be nine feet long pointing straight out from his upper jaw. It is the ivory spear which Eskimos use.

Many species of dolphins roam the seas. Some are called

bottle-nosed; some have a mouth that looks like the beak of a bird. Smaller than the dolphins are the porpoises. Sleek and black, they tumble about in the waves as though at play. Sailors call them sea pigs and harpoon them for their flesh which is like beef.

Porpoises love to swim about ships. In New Zealand, for many years, a famous dolphin named Pelorus Jack used to meet incoming vessels and escort them into the harbor. The government passed a law to protect him.

Some dolphins and porpoises have left the sea to live in rivers and even in some lakes. One species of dolphin is found only in the Ganges, the sacred river of India, where he has become almost blind in those muddy waters.

There are other animals that seem quite at home on sea or shore. Among these are the seals. Some are hunted for their flesh and their hides. But the most famous are the seals whose warm fur is used for costly coats.

These seals are found in summer on the tiny group of islands called the Pribilofs in the Bering Sea. Here mother seals go to have their babies, and seal families stay for several months. The youngsters play about on the beach or in the surf. Dense fogs shield them from the hot sun. Several million seals gather there, and their barking and yelping can be heard for miles.

Killers will attack a large whale like a pack of wolves.

When September gales whip the waves, the seals go back to the sea. It is thought that they seek their food along the edges of the continental shelves where the shallows slope down to the deep sea. For strange fish that live there have been found in their stomachs. Like whales, seals can dive far down into the sea, but all must come to the surface to breathe.

All About the Sea

Another land animal quite at home in the sea is the walrus. Two great teeth hang from his upper jaw. These may be more than thirty inches long and weigh fifteen pounds. With them the walrus pulls himself out on a floating ice cake for a nap in the sun. And with them he digs the rocky beaches for clams and other shellfish which are his food.

We would not expect a bear to go to sea. But the white bear of the Arctic seems quite at home on the waves. He has been found swimming more than twenty miles from shore, where he went chasing seals or fish. His thick white coat keeps him warm. Except the great brown bear of Alaska, he is the largest of all the bears. For he may

Two seals watch a walrus pull himself out on floating ice.

weigh 1,600 pounds. Bears farther south sleep through the winter. But the white bear has no place to go, no cave or other shelter. And so he braves the cruel frost and winds through the long darkness of the Arctic night.

Warmer waters have other creatures that we would not care to meet on land or sea. They are water snakes of many colors, black, yellow or green. They may grow to a length of six feet or more. Some have poison fangs more deadly than those of a rattlesnake. Fortunately, they are found only in tropic waters and are not common even there.

Birds That Love the Spray

Scientists divide the birds into two great groups—land birds and water birds. And of the water birds many are true lovers of the sea. Their feet are webbed to serve as paddles; their feathers are waterproofed. They are never happy far from the roar of the surf or the smell of the salt spray.

Wildest and freest of all sea birds is the albatross. One big member of this family may have a wingspread of eleven feet or more. Though his body is rather heavy, he is the champion of long-distance flyers. He will follow a ship for days, soaring through the air and seldom even moving his wings. He seems the very spirit of lonely seas. To cross the ocean is sport for him. Sailors claim that he can sleep on the wing. Certainly he can ride the waves better than any boat and rise into the air when he pleases. As the ship he follows nears the land, he will turn away and follow another ship out into the sea. Albatrosses only go ashore to lay their eggs and rear their young. The sea is their home.

Even more graceful than the albatross is the frigate bird of tropic seas. His scythe-like wings may measure seven and a half feet across. His long tail is split like that of a swallow. He circles through the air without effort and seems to love flying. But he is a great robber and makes slower birds share their catch of fish with him.

Most sea birds are fishermen. Perhaps the most skillful is the cormorant. In swimming under water he uses both wings and feet. One was caught in a crab trap 120 feet below the surface. Japanese tame cormorants to fish for them. They put a collar around the cormorant's neck so he cannot swallow the fish which they take from him.

A strange sea bird is the puffin. He is short and squat with a white shirt front and a black coat. His big beak is striped with yellow, blue and red. He looks as though he were wearing a mask. No wonder sailors call him the

Albatross (left); cormorant (center); and the frigate bird.

sea parrot. But his beak is useful in catching fish and in digging holes in the bank where he makes his nest.

Much better known are the gulls and terns. Though true sea birds they are often found over fresh water lakes. Gulls feed on dead fish along tidal beaches. Because of this useful work, they are protected by law.

Terns, which are smaller birds, are expert divers. Fishermen often watch terns, and when they see them plunging into the water they know fish are there. One species called the Arctic tern builds her nest in summer in the Far North, then flies 11,000 miles or more to winter in Antarctica. She must love sunlight more than any other creature. Eight months out of the year she spends in places where the sun never sets.

Still more wonderful is the flight of the golden plover. From Alaska he wings his way to Hawaii, a distance of

The golden plover (left) and the sandpiper love the sea.

Tern (upper left); stormy petrel (left); and sea gulls.

2,400 miles. How he ever finds those islands in the vast Pacific is a mystery.

A queer looking water bird is the pelican, "whose beak holds more than his belly can." A big bird, he may have a wingspread of ten feet or more. He looks clumsy. But he can give points to our best divers as he hits the waves and plunges under after a fish that he has seen from the air. On some islands along the South American coasts he gathers in what might be called bird cities. These are great gatherings of birds that may number a million or more. In such islands off Peru it is thought that pelicans catch and eat a thousand tons of fish a day.

The stormy petrels are pretty little sea birds. Sailors named them that for they think they appear before storms. They are also called Mother Carey's chickens. In small groups they skim above the waves as though in play. And they are found hundreds of miles from land.

Many shore birds get their living from the sea. Among these are the sandpipers. They race along the edge of the surf on sandy beaches. There they pick up tiny shrimp-like creatures that the waves uncover. Though small, they can run very fast.

In the rocky islands along the coast of Scotland men gather sea-bird eggs for food. The Eskimos in the Far North depend upon little birds called dovekies. They dip them out of the air in hand nets as one might catch fish. Many dovekies are stored for winter food while warm shirts are made from their downy skins.

Oddest of all are the sea birds which cannot fly. Such are the penguins which are found chiefly in Antarctica. Their wings have become rubbery fins which help them dart about under water chasing fish. Seeing men but seldom, they have no fear and are friendly. They stand erect, bowing and making queer noises as though they were

Of all birds, penguins seem most like human beings.

talking. Of all birds they seem most like human beings. Usually they wear white shirt fronts and black coats.

But the largest of the penguins, called the Emperor, has a golden shirt front. He may stand nearly four feet tall and weigh eighty-five pounds. When a scientist tried to capture one, the bird knocked him down and jumped on his chest. Living in the world's worst climate, they hatch their young under snowdrifts. But they do not mind the cold and the storms, for they have never known anything else.

Many land birds sometimes put to sea. Wild geese often do this when they go south in winter. They fly in a V-shaped group. At the head is a wise old gander. He has made many such journeys and knows all the best stopping places. You may have heard wild geese in flight, honking like distant autos.

Even humming birds, smallest of all the birds, fly 500 miles across the Gulf of Mexico to Central and South America.

These are but a few of the birds that get their food from the sea or cross it on long journeys to distant lands.

The Sea and Man

Farming the Sea

We live in a crowded world. In many countries people go hungry because there isn't food enough or good land to grow it on. And the number who must be fed increases all the time. So in many places men have turned to farming the sea.

On land our fruits and vegetables are wild plants that have been improved. Potatoes were once only poor roots. Wheat and rice were mere grass seed. Farmers have learned through many years how to grow better apples and strawberries. Through 4-H Clubs, boys and girls have learned to raise finer pigs and chickens. But they cannot learn how to grow better herrings or great blue whales.

For all that, we should reap richer harvests from the sea. There are the seaweeds that cover the rocks at low tide and the kelp jungles in deep water. In France, Scotland and Norway such seaweeds have been gathered for hundreds of years. They are pulled from the rocks by hand or cut by scythes on long poles. Great machines are now pushed through beds of giant kelp that can reap twenty-five tons in an hour. Such weed makes good fertilizer for crops on land. Asparagus thrives with seaweed at its roots, and seed potatoes wrapped in seaweed will grow fine crops that are free from scab.

Seaweed is also burned for its valuable ashes. The iodine you may have put on a cut finger was first obtained from seaweed. The mineral called potassium was found in the potash of burned kelp.

From a red seaweed, scientists get a substance that disease germs feed upon. Doctors study these germs to learn how to treat them. Many useful drugs are obtained from seaweed. Yet thousands of tons wash ashore every year only to be wasted.

All About the Sea

We might not think that seaweed was worth much as food. Yet in the markets of our eastern states a red kind called *dulse* is often sold. Many people like to chew dulse, and in Scotland they stew it in milk. Another seaweed, Irish moss, grows along the rocky coasts of New England and elsewhere. It is of many colors—cream, red, yellow, green and almost black. Made into a pudding, it is delicious.

Other countries make better use of what the sea has to give them. The Japanese get nearly half their food from the sea. Much of this is fish and shellfish, but some thirty different kinds of seaweed are also eaten. These appear in soups, vegetable dishes and even candy. Do not smile, for the ice cream you like so well may have been thickened with a substance obtained from seaweed.

The Japanese are crowded into rocky islands too small to support them. But they have a long coastline with many bays and shallows where seaweeds thrive. You would also find seaweeds eaten along the coasts of China and the Philippines. In markets there, it is piled in golden heaps like maple sugar.

Seaweeds are the only vegetable food the Eskimos ever have. At the southern tip of South America there once lived a tribe of Indians called Kelp Eaters. That was because most of their food came from the great kelp beds of the stormy sea.

All these are plants that grow wild in the sea. But seaweeds have been planted, too. In Ireland flat stones are laid down in shallow water to catch the spores of seaweed which are something like the seeds of land plants. When the weed is grown, it is cut off and the stone turned over to catch a new crop. In Japan bushes are set out over thousands of acres of shallow sea water to catch a red seaweed. The crop is harvested in winter from January to March, and the bushes are made ready for a new crop.

Animal life in the sea is much harder to control. But sponges, which are lowly animals, have been raised like cucumbers. Slabs of concrete are laid down with bits of sponge attached. When full grown, they are scraped off and the slabs prepared for a new crop. Imitation sponges are now made of rubber, but these are not quite so good for some purposes as those grown in the sea.

Oysters are raised for market much like other crops. Shells are scattered in shallow waters to catch the baby oysters which swim about. Each grows a tiny shell. As they cling to larger shells, they look much like freckles. Soon they become "seed oysters" which are taken up and scattered over shallow bays or inlets.

Oysters are cultivated, too. For like corn or tomatoes they have many enemies. Sometimes they are transplanted to other beds to improve their flavor. In northern waters full-grown oysters may be four or five years old.

Men have also tried to raise lobsters as they might raise chickens in fenced pens. Only these pens are in shallow

Lobsters are savage fighters.

sea water. Millions of tiny lobsters have been hatched from the egg and set free. Lobsters are savage though you might not think so. They are always fighting, and like cannibals they attack and eat one another.

In Japan much progress has been made in growing pearls. Pearl oysters and other shellfish sometimes make these lovely gems. When a grain of sand or other matter gets between their shells, they cover its rough edges with nacre which is the substance of pearls. They do this to protect themselves. And so in Japan bits of different shapes are thrust between the shells of living shellfish which turn out pearls almost to order.

These are only a few ways in which men are learning to farm the seas. So far they have made only a beginning. You should see great progress in this field and perhaps will help to bring it about.

Mining the Sea

The wealth of the sea goes beyond mere plants and animals. It includes rich deposits of minerals. We find that the sea has been mined ever since men first learned to scrape salt from the rocks where it had been left by the ebb tide.

All About the Sea

In many parts of the world salt is still gathered in much the same way. Sea water is allowed to flow into shallow reservoirs where it dries out in the warm air. The salt is then piled in heaps to bleach in the sun. Such salt is rather coarse and gray.

The salt which we use on our tables is mined on land. In some places it has collected under the rocks in layers half a mile thick. In other places there are reservoirs of brine deep in the earth's crust. Both mines and reservoirs are the remains of seas that once covered the land. The seas have gone and left their salt behind, or they have been buried deep in the earth. Wherever we get our salt, we are mining the sea.

There are other minerals in the sea besides salt. Every cubic mile of sea water holds over 150 million tons of minerals. One of the most valuable is iodine. Another is bromine. Over nine-tenths of all the bromine in the world is in the sea. Bromine is used in photographic plates and in many remedies the drug stores sell.

Some of the minerals we get from the sea are sprinkled on our roads to lay the dust. They are also used in making cement and rubber and many plastics. One big company now makes over five hundred different things out of minerals from the sea.

Aluminum is useful for kitchen pots and pans and for airplanes. That is because it is so much lighter than iron or steel and does not rust. But there is another common metal even lighter than aluminum. It is magnesium. Henry Ford thought this metal would be used more and more in automobiles. He even believed that it might become the metal of the future, just as iron might be called the metal of today.

If so, we shall do much more mining of the sea. For the sea is the great source of magnesium. Sea water is now being drawn into reservoirs or vats where oyster shells are piled in heaps. The magnesium in the water joins the lime in the oyster shells and is separated later.

Many oil wells have been drilled in shallow waters offshore.

All About the Sea

Petroleum, which gives us fuel oil and kerosene and gasoline, is also thought to be a gift from the sea. Long ages ago millions upon millions of tiny living things, the plankton of ancient seas, collected in great beds. As the continents rose, these beds were buried by sand and clay that turned to rock. The oil in these plants and animals remained deep down underground.

Today we drill wells to these deposits, and the petroleum gushes out in springs or is pumped up like water. Some of these wells are thousands of feet deep. Some have even been driven through shallow waters many miles from shore.

Yes, men are now mining the sea or places where the sea has been. They will depend more and more upon the sea. For it is a great storehouse where untold mineral wealth has collected for hundreds of millions of years.

Sailing the Seas

When men first sailed the seas, they kept within sight of land. For if they went too far from shore, how could they know where they were?

But today the captain of a ship knows just where he is. He can take a map and put his finger upon the very spot.

He estimates it by the distance from two other places. One of these is the equator; the other is a city in England called Greenwich. The equator is a line around the earth halfway between the North and South Poles.

The captain has an instrument called a *sextant*. This instrument gives him the height of the sun above the horizon. And from that height he can measure his distance north of the equator. This is known as *latitude*.

The captain has another instrument called a *chronometer*. It gives him the time at Greenwich. If he is sailing in the Pacific, he knows it was noontime in Greenwich long before it was noon in the Pacific. And that difference in time tells him how far he is from Greenwich. This is called *longitude*.

And now the captain knows all that he needs to know. He has his distance north of the equator. He has his distance west of Greenwich. He can draw two lines upon the map, and they meet where his ship now is. Give the captain the latitude and longitude of any place on earth, and he can locate it for you.

There is another instrument the captain uses which is quite as important as the sextant and chronometer. It is called a compass. Boy Scouts carry a compass to find their direction in the woods. Big ships now have a special kind which points always toward the North Pole. The man who is steering the ship at sea watches the compass to be sure that he is going in the right direction.

And he has another instrument to guide him too. It is called the *log*. This trails behind the ship and measures its speed through the water. The captain knows how far he traveled since the day before and in what direction.

When the sun is hidden for days or the ship carried far off its course by storms, the captain uses what he calls "dead reckoning." He estimates the strength of winds and ocean currents. And if he is a good navigator, he is not far wrong. Fishing ships, groping through fog on the Grand Banks, often depend upon "dead reckoning."

The skilled navigator studies the surface of the sea, its waves and tides and currents. But he must also know something about the bottom. In mid-ocean he may be miles out of his way and no great harm result. As he nears the shore, he must be more careful. For reefs and rocks and sand bars may mean shipwreck.

In the old days sailing ships often let down a lead weight upon a cord to find how deep the water was. They called this "sounding." But sailors have a language of their own. They called it "heaving the lead" or "flying the blue pigeon." Sometimes they also wished to know what kind of bottom lay beneath them. And so they greased the lead and examined the mud or sand or shells that stuck to it.

To aid ships the governments of most countries make maps of the shallow waters along their coasts. These are called *charts*. Land maps often give the height above sea level. Charts give the depth below. Many rocks are scattered along the shore that never show above the waves. These must also be marked upon the chart so that ships may avoid them.

In a storm a ship may be carried off its course.

The shore is always dangerous to a ship. In storms ships hurry to reach land if the captain can find a safe harbor. If not, he tries to work his way back to the open sea. A stout ship can fight the winds and waves, but it cannot fight rocks or sand bars.

Because shore lines are always changing, charts must be brought up to date. Besides, dangerous rocks are being discovered all the time.

Charts near shore are drawn in much the same way as land maps. The airplane has made this far easier than it used to be. From an airplane you can look through shallow water and see all the rocks that lie upon the bottom. And so, with airplane cameras we now have charts that are becoming more and more accurate.

In olden times men feared to sail the seas at night. They tried to reach some harbor where they could wait for the day. But even then some lights shone out from shore to guide ships on their way.

Now many lighthouses have been placed on dangerous rocks far out at sea. Here the keepers have been held prisoners by storms for weeks or even months.

Lighthouse keepers learn much about the power of waves in a storm. The first lighthouse built on Minot's Ledge off the Massachusetts coast was swept away, and

Lighthouses have been placed on dangerous rocks at sea.

the keepers drowned. Tillamook Rock off Oregon is 112 feet high. Yet waves have climbed that rock and hurled big stones through the lighthouse windows far above. Even higher is North Unst Rock north of Scotland. But a big wave once swept up that rock for 196 feet and smashed in a half-ton door as if it had been paper.

Building lighthouses on distant rocks has often proved a hard task. To place a lighthouse on sandy shoals may be even more difficult. Rocks give a firm base, but sands may shift with every storm. Our government has tried several times to build a lighthouse on Diamond Shoals off Cape Hatteras. But the attempts failed and a lightship was put there instead. Many other lightships are anchored in places where no lighthouses can be built.

Most lighthouses give out a white light. But some are red, green and even blue. Most are fixed lights; others turn continually about. They are all marked on charts so that ships watching for lights as they near the shore can tell where they are.

Many harbors have buoys to guide ships safely in. Buoys are of many kinds. Some are little more than stakes usually painted red or black. Many are made of iron. They are hollow and float. They are anchored so they will not drift about. Some have bells that ring as the waves rise and fall. Some have lights that flash. Some have hoarse whistles that can be heard for miles. Many lighthouses have fog horns that sound when fog settles down upon the water.

Today lighthouses are not needed so much as they once

were. Many have no keepers, for their lights are controlled by electricity. Most big ships now carry radios and keep in touch with shore stations. Radio beams show a captain, even in a dense fog, just where he is. Radio reports also give warning of storms and winds and tides. And so man is learning to conquer the perils of the sea.

How the Sea Controls Our Climate

In summer millions of people go to the seashore. They like the bathing and boating and fishing. But they also enjoy the cool breezes that blow in upon the hot land. For the sea largely controls what we call our climate.

In the first place, the sea covers nearly three-quarters of the earth. But it also has a steadying influence upon the dry land. For it keeps the air from becoming too hot or too cold as well as too dry.

Many of our houses have what is called a *thermostat.* This little gadget hanging upon the wall can regulate the heat in winter. If you want your rooms warmer or cooler, you merely change the thermostat. The sea serves as a vast thermostat for the whole world.

On land the temperature may go as low as 94 degrees below zero. In the African desert it may go as high as 136 degrees above zero. That is a difference of 230 degrees.

There are no such differences in ocean temperatures. The warmest of all ocean water is in the Gulf of Persia where it reaches 96 degrees above zero. The coldest is along parts of the ocean floor where it has sunk to about 27. This is a difference of less than 70 degrees. Most surface waters vary but a few degrees from July to January, while the waters below the surface vary scarcely at all.

This is because water is heated or cooled far more slowly than air. It takes about 3,000 times as much heat to heat a quart of water as it does a quart of air. It takes a long time for spring suns to warm the winter seas. It takes a long time for autumn frosts to chill the summer

One of the earliest sailing vessels was a raft ship.

seas. And so the seacoasts have late springs and autumns while summers are cooler and winters warmer than in places farther inland.

There are other reasons why the sea has so much influence upon our climates. There are those great rivers of the sea called ocean currents. They carry the warmth of tropic seas far to the north and south. They bear the chill of Polar Seas toward the equator. Because of warm ocean currents daffodils bloom in winter in southern England and roses in Oregon. Cold ocean currents chill Labrador and Maine and make a desert of the seacoast of Peru. In many countries the climate is almost entirely controlled by ocean currents.

But most important of all are the clouds that drift inland from the sea and the rains that fall upon the parched ground. For the sea, as we have noted, is the source of that moisture which sustains all life everywhere.

You may have heard old people say the climate is getting warmer. They claim that we no longer have the hard winters they knew when they were young. And they may be right. For in mountain regions those rivers of ice we call glaciers seem to be slowly melting.

In any case, scientists know that the world has been much warmer and much colder than it is today. They know that it has been warmer, for fig trees and magnolias once grew in Greenland and there are great seams of coal in Antarctica where a few lichens are the only plant life now. And they also know it was once much colder. For great ice fields overspread Canada and stretched south below the Ohio River. In places this ice was probably two miles thick and covered many of the mountain peaks. And there were ice fields also in Europe and Asia.

Those great ice fields have been melting for 20,000 years. But they have not wholly gone. They cover almost all of Antarctica and Greenland and some lesser islands. There are places in Greenland where the ice is still nearly 8,000 feet thick. More than one-tenth of all the land surface of the earth, even now, is buried deep in ice.

Nor is that all. There is reason to believe that these great ice fields advanced and then retreated several times during the past million years. And going back for hundreds of millions of years other ice fields also spread and then melted away. They carried great rocks long distances. They carved deep valleys and built up hills. Much of our landscape still bears the scars of ice that melted long ago.

What causes such great changes in the world's climate still puzzles scientists. Some believe that at certain times volcanoes have poured so much dust into the upper air that the sun's rays were cut down. We know how a cloud passing over the sun cools the air on a hot day. Clouds of volcanic dust might cool the whole world.

Other scientists have thought that the earth itself wobbled upon its axis just as a spinning top will do as it comes to rest. Such motions would throw the seasons off balance and change the climate.

Some have wondered if the sun, dragging the earth with it as it journeys on through space, may not drift through great clouds of star dust. These would cut down its rays and chill the earth.

Whatever caused these changes in climate they have had a great effect upon the sea as well as the dry land. If all the ice in Greenland and Antarctica should suddenly melt, the surface of the sea would rise perhaps a hundred feet or more. New York and London and all other seaports would then be under water. The Mississippi Valley would once more become an ocean gulf.

Or suppose another ice age should come like that of 20,000 years ago. Then so much water would be taken out of the sea that its surface would be lowered everywhere. Asia and North America would join once more, and the British Isles would become a part of Europe.

All About the Sea

We need not worry about such changes, for they come about very slowly through thousands or perhaps millions of years. They have occurred and will probably occur again. And as we learn more about them we can better understand the story of our world and of the sea.

Lovely Presents From the Sea

When we visit the seashore, we like to pick up a few of the shells we find there. In many old New England homes there are queer shells. They were brought back from China or the Far East, long ago, in some great clipper ship. Some museums have millions of such shells.

Shells are grown by a great family of creatures that scientists call *mollusks*. Next to the insects, they are the most numerous of living things. They have soft bodies and most of them develop shells as a kind of outside skeleton or as a shield against their enemies.

Most mollusks have but a single shell. Some have left the sea and prefer the land. The snails you find in your garden are mollusks. They are fond of plants.

There are land snails in Africa that weigh several pounds. But much larger ones live in the sea. One species off the Florida coast grows to be two feet long. An even

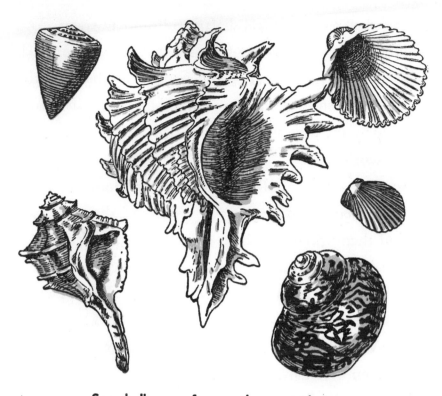

Sea shells are of many shapes and sizes.

larger species is found in the Pacific. It weighs as much as twenty-five pounds.

The shell is really the creature's house. In building it he often shows great skill. The chambered nautilus has a house with many rooms. But he lives in only one of them. As he gets larger, he builds a larger room and moves into it, walling up the old one behind him. The rooms are all arranged around a central shaft in a beautiful spiral. And he lines them with a kind of plaster that glows like pearl.

In another species called the paper nautilus only the mother has a shell in which to carry her eggs and young. Rocked by the waves it has been called the loveliest cradle in the world.

Some snail-like mollusks have a trap door for their shells. When afraid they crawl inside and shut the door behind them. Some of these doors are so beautiful that natives in the Far East use them for jewelry.

Other mollusks have shells with many spikes. That is so hungry fishes will not nibble at them. One of these is called Venus' Comb. If you chose, you could use it to comb your own hair.

Many mollusks have two shells. They fit together like the hinge of a door. Some of these mollusks are as tiny as bird shot. The largest is the so-called giant clam which abounds along the Great Australian Reef. When grown, he may weigh 600 pounds or more. He is too heavy to move, and so he lies upon his back with his shells partly open. His flesh is highly colored and may be green or almost black. Native pearl divers, groping along the bottom in the dim light, sometimes thrust a hand between his shells. These close and the poor diver is caught, as in a bear trap, and drowns. And so this mollusk has been called the Man Eating Clam. He isn't really, for he is only trying to protect himself.

Many shells are used for various purposes. Some make fine dishes and ash trays and drinking horns. On Pacific islands the natives use them as lamps and even tea kettles. In the Philippines window panes are sometimes made of shell. So are horns and trumpets. Fishermen on the Grand Banks blow a conch shell to warn passing ships in the fog. In India a certain kind of shell is used as a trumpet in temple services. It is a holy object in the Hindu religion. Giant clam shells have been placed in Catholic churches and filled with holy water.

Shells have often been used as jewels. Cameos are carved from conch shells which grow in the Mediterranean. Finest of all shell products are pearls. For they are made of the same substance and in much the same way as other shells. They have been called the dew drops of the sea, for they reflect every color of the rainbow. Unlike diamonds and rubies which must be cut and ground, the pearl is the one perfect gem in all nature.

Shells have often served as money. The Indians had wampum made from shells. In Africa and some other parts of the world shells still pass for money. In the Fiji

All About the Sea

Islands a certain kind of shell was given by the chiefs as a badge of merit.

Some shells are very rare. There is one in the British Museum which is the only known specimen. Another conelike shell is called the Glory of the Seas. Only about a dozen have ever been found. Many shells are worth several dollars. Some are worth hundreds of dollars.

Most people pick up shells because of their strange shape or color. Yet they know little about the mollusks that made them. Hold a big shell to your ear, and you may hear a murmur like the sea. But you would hear more wonderful stories if you listened to the life and habits of the creature that made that shell.

Perhaps you have wished that you might have sailed with Columbus to discover a new world. But there is a new world lying all about you and in fancy you can take a much longer voyage than his. You can learn more about the sea than Columbus ever knew. And learning about it is a voyage of adventure that can last as long as you live.

Index

Index

Index